Introductory note

It is all about the intersection of fate, decision and chance. And politics. And music. And..

I graduated in History and Politics in 1980. The Chancellor of the Exchequer of the era, the name escapes me – was entirely responsible for my immediate lack of employment. For the first time I can remember I was at home in the afternoon, the sort of time when it is too early or too late to do something world changing, at least that day, the sort of age when you can't listen *entirely* to The Rolling Stones or The Pretenders. Moving the radio dial around with the sound of international static I almost expected to come across General De Gaulle's call to the Free French or an original Reith lecture. '…hand you back to the studio from a rain swept Headingley to rejoin our colleagues in the studio for Afternoon Theatre.' Fate, decision?

With an aptness seeming beyond chance the play that day was a dramatization partly based on Anthony Powell's Afternoon Men. My afternoons changed completely. So did the Chancellor.

It was 2002 before I completed a draft of my first radio play on a Kindertransport theme, Roundhay Ringstrasse. The title reflected my own background, born In Leeds, my father a Yorkshire man, my mother originally from Vienna. They lived in the Roundhay district of Leeds after their marriage. The feedback was encouraging, the play jejune, but the train of thought moving in the right direction. The two plays in this volume are attempts to come to terms with the Kindertransport theme in my own way in a dramatic fiction medium with research that would at least meet the standards of a History and Politics graduate on a dry afternoon years after both my parents, and that nameless Chancellor, had long departed.

It's never too late.

1 Vienna, love (screenplay)

2 Platform Free (simple stage version from radio format)

(TV and radio versions of Roundhay Ringstrasse are included in Drama King*)

3 Bibliographical review

Vienna, Love

By

John F King

ISBN 9780955851971

Ilkley / Leeds HMD 2014

www.johnkingcommunications.co.uk

www.johnkinginternational.eu

www.secondgeneration.org.uk

With love and thanks to

Angela Despina, on a special birthday
2014

Picture above, John King and Angela Despina at London Liverpool Street station on 75th anniversary of the Kindertransport, 1.12.2013

Picture below of my mother and father Elsie and Terry Fagan, 1951 (Elsie, née Ilse Hölzelmacher came from Vienna to Yorkshire by Kindertransport, 1939.)

ISBN 9780955851971

Vienna, Love.

John F King

'You do not have to suffer to learn. But if you don't learn from suffering over which you have no control then your life becomes truly meaningless.'

Viktor Frankl. Man's Search for Meaning.

VIENNA, LOVE

By

John F King

York European Publishing

VIENNA, LOVE is set mainly in Vienna and Leeds immediately before, during and after the Second World War. The ages indicated for the cast are as at 1938, just before the German annexation of Austria.

VIENNA

STERN Family:

JOSEF father

HELENE mother to Ilse

ILSE (later ElSIE), 15

HENRYK, 12

AUGE Family:

JACOB father

MAGDA mother to GRETA

GRETA, 14

WERNER, 17 from Berlin, apprentice to JOSEF

LEEDS

TERENCE LAMBERT father

INGRID mother to TEDDY (EDWARD)

TEDDY (EDWARD), 16

CYNTHIA, 16

MAVIS,16 and HEADMISTRESS, Leeds High School for Girls

Plus The TREGOWANS, police, officials etc.

On radio: newsreels, dance music

Music♪ for titles, on radio, in performance by

Brahms, Delibes, Mendelssohn, Schubert, Strauss J, Reich S…

EXT. LEEDS STATION - DAY

Smartly dressed now elderly TEDDY is awaiting commuter train home at modern Leeds station. Looks at watch and platform display board. His train is pulling in. Electrical display board shorts out and clock stops. The carriage which halts directly in front of him is a 1940s cattle truck, the doors open as from within, inside scenes of devastation, dead bodies, including children, buckets etc, doors close from within, the train leaves, clock starts again, display board shows:

'TITLE'

EXT. STREET OUTSIDE STERN'S WORKSHOP - NIGHT

Vienna District 2, November 1938, street view. Trams pass, across the street through a workshop window a light shines. Worklamp shadow of JOSEF working on an intricate instrument. A shaft of light indicates a door opening into the room, a silhouette - a young girl ILSE -enters. Immediately the worklamp is switched off. The workshop is now illuminated by street lamps and the light from the door. Josef places a work drape over the work station before the girl can discover what he is working on. He points to the door making an upstairs gesture. Reluctantly she leaves through the door. He checks round the workshop and follows her upstairs into

INTERCUT

INT. THE STERN'S LIVING ROOM ABOVE THE WORKSHOP - SAME NIGHT

The rumble of trams can still be heard. It is a comfortable room, books, piano, family pictures in photos and paintings, including wedding photo, photo of Josef in First World War Austrian Army uniform, photos of children, painting of London etc.

HELENE is at her fine desk writing a letter, the Leeds address on the envelope is visible. As soon as Ilse enters Helene stops and closes desk lid.

ILSE

Secrets!

Josef enters the room after her. She turns to him then her mother.

ILSE

Secrets, this family has secrets and you said..

JOSEF

There are no secrets in this family.

ILSE

You are keeping something from me.

HELENE

We are not keeping anything from you, darling.

JOSEF

You are keeping us all from our beds, young lady

ILSE

Let me stay up, at least until mother has finished the programme. My first official concert. One day I'll decorate my apartment with them. I can see it now, Hyde Park, the Albert Hall, I won't need a chauffeur I can walk to work!

HELENE

Your talent is dreaming when you haven't - won't - go to bed. Come on, my girl.

ILSE

Just let me see a programme, at least the cover, then I'll go to bed. P-R-O-M-I-S-E.

JOSEF

Ilse, you need to look promise up in your school dictionary, precise definition.

ILSE

Just the cover.

Josef and Helene look at each other.

HELENE

Close your eyes.

As Ilse closes her eyes Helene carefully reopens the desk. She moves the letter she was writing and other documents away from view then pulls out the cover of a programme. It is very skilfully decorated. Helene looks back at Josef.

JOSEF

Open.

Ilse takes the programme.

ILSE

Oh Mother, it is beautiful.

(she kisses her mother.) Beautiful.

(she reads from the programme) '…on the occasion of her birthday the Ilse Stern Trio…'

JOSEF

The Ilse Stern trio. A trio isn't a one man band, young lady.

HELENE

Or a young lady band, my man.

ILSE

One day I'll be a soloist, I won't need anyone else.

JOSEF

One day…

ILSE

(Continuing reading)

'perform for esteemed guests, friends and family…And we welcome to our home Werner Vogel from Berlin..' Does he have to be on our programme, that..that what is that abbreviation

N -A -Z -I.

HELENE

Ilse that is enough. Time.

Ilse stares at them both for a moment. The stares are held. Then gives her parents a goodnight kiss, Ilse exits door opposite.

Helene returns programme to desk, closes lid and locks it, gives key to Josef.

HELENE

Is he?

JOSEF

Is he, who, what?

HELENE

You know perfectly well what I mean, Mr Master Craftsman Stern.

JOSEF

I wouldn't even know what N A Z I means. I don't know and I don't care, I don't hire artisans for politics, I only hire the best.

HELENE

And best right now is bed.

JOSEF

I'll be up shortly, darling.

Helene gives him a look and exits. Josef checks the desk and switches off desk light. He leaves through same door as he came in. From street view he re-enters workshop. As street lamps go off the workshop lamp goes back on.

EXT. PERIMETER RAF TRAINING STATION - MORNING

Near Leeds 1938. Cycle leaning against fence. Young Teddy watching aircraft take off and land. He enters notes in his notebook, eventually cycles off, past allotments, terraced houses. Enters terrace house.

TEDDY

It's me.

TERENCE, Teddy's dad is finishing breakfast. Mum INGRID hands him briefcase. He checks papers / charts inside, closes briefcase firmly.

TEDDY

Dad?

TERENCE

Not now, son

TEDDY

Dad?

TERENCE

Anything changed between yesterday and today? The answer is No.

TEDDY

Dad..

INGRID

Did you not understand your father.

She kisses father goodbye, he takes hat and leaves for work using their tandem bicycle.

TEDDY

Mum?

INGRID

Don't be pushing your father, son. He has a lot on.

No means no.

TEDDY

(At door,shouts after departing father)

Dad!

INGRID

Inside, Edward now. I – we've- had enough of this. Eat your breakfast. We try our best for you and this is the thanks given to us.

TEDDY

Not hungry. I'll cycle into school.

Looks at his cycle, looks up at an overhead aircraft stalling, alarming silence, Teddy and mother look at each other, then aero engine splutters and restarts. Teddy walks off.

INGRID

(calls after him)

Son, (her accent slips) Sohn..

EXT. BERLIN MAIN STATION - MORNING

WERNER VOGEL, 17, very smartly dressed in new suit walking to station approach. National Socialist activists are handing out leaflets in morning rush hour, mixed reactions, Werner is ignored but picks up a leaflet that another passer by threw away in disgust. Enters platform where Vienna express is announced. As he is asked for his ticket, he puts leaflet into his pocket, presents travel document to rail travel official

OFFICIAL

Vienna, you are very young for an international journey.

WERNER

Vienna, international?

OFFICIAL

Purpose of your journey?

WERNER

I will be apprentice to the best musical instrument maker in the world.

INT. JOSEF STERN'S WORKSHOP - SAME MORNING

Josef has fallen asleep at his workplace, the lamp is still on. His wife enters, switches off lamp. Thinks of waking him but lets him be. Leaves a breakfast basket, gives him a kiss. As she turns to leave Ilse enters.

ILSE

Good morning, Mother. Is everything ready for the concert?

HELENE

Good morning, Ilse. Thank you I am very well.

Please close the door quietly, you'll wake your father.

ILSE

Why is father sleeping in the workshop?

JOSEF

Ilse, what are you doing in the workshop so late?

HELENE

Poor father. Good morning dearest.

JOSEF

Good morning, darling, good morning Ilse.

ILSE

Good morning, father. I must be going.

JOSEF

Ilse, I would like to ask you to do something for me.

ILSE

Father, I'll be late for my lessons.

HELENE

Ilse

ILSE

Yes, of course, what is it?

JOSEF

Young Herr Vogel will arrive at Vienna main station at 4pm this afternoon. I want you to meet him.

ILSE

Me?

JOSEF

Is there someone else in the room called Ilse?

ILSE

But, my rehearsal.

JOSEF.

This is business, you are old enough to represent the family. Meet him under the clock on the main concourse and bring him here to the workshop, his new place of work. You can continue your rehearsal later.

ILSE

But, father

Ilse's brother HENRYK has entered.

JOSEF

Ilse, main concourse, 4 pm. I am counting on you Ilse.

ILSE

Why me?

HENRYK

I'll go.

JOSEF

Thank you, Henryk but your..

HENRYK

My eyes are much better now, I can easily go and meet the Berlin train.

HELENE

Henryk.

JOSEF

Thank you, son. I am not asking you to meet the Berlin train. I am asking your sister to meet Herr Vogel as a courtesy. Ilse, kindly indicate you will do as I - mother and I - request.

ILSE

Very well.

She leaves, knocking over a music stand.

INT. TEDDY'S FAMILY HOUSE - LATER THAT AFTERNOON

Radio on, Ingrid listening to BBC news, laying table, preparing fresh veg. Teddy enters whistling dance tune, walks directly to wireless and retunes it to dance programme, playing the same tune he is whistling.

INGRID

Edward, if you don't mind young man I was listening to the news.

TEDDY

Doom and gloom. What time is tea?

INGRID

Tea time is when your father gets in.

Letter for you, funny stamps.

TEDDY

Collects letter from mantelpiece

Good old Henry.

INGRID

I thought his name was Henryk.

TEDDY

Henry, Henryk, you know that. I'll see what the old boy is on about this week.

INGRID

Trains, Planes, Trains, planes, about time you ' old boys' were girl spotting, I wouldn't wonder.

TEDDY

Shouldn't

INGRID

Shouldn't?

TEDDY

I shouldn't wonder

INGRID

Shouldn't be any tea for you if you are not careful.

Teddy goes upstairs into his room. Radio station retuned to news, sound audible downstairs although words cannot be made out. His room is a den: models of trains, planes hanging from ceiling, on wall pictures of pilots, cricketers etc, no pictures of girls, map of Europe. He traces a flight line from Vienna to Leeds.

Teddy opens the envelope, saving the stamps

HENRYK (V.O)

'My dear Teddy, I am sorry I have not written for a while. We have been so busy rehearsing for the big concert, now nearly upon us. I am playing the piano.

I have had some problems with my eyes so I have to play with - is that right - memory as much as I can. As I said please be free to correct my English. My sister and I are having extra lessons at school. I hope you can tell the difference since my last letter.

Yes, yes I know you will be impatient, I know you are really only interested in trains and planes though sometimes you pretend otherwise. By the time you read this our guest Werner will be arriving by express train from Berlin to Vienna. What a great journey!

Maybe one day we could do it together. I’ll ask Werner Vogel what aeroplanes he has seen in Germany. Here is an article about a new designer, Herr Messerschmitt, it says he will be working on the fastest plane in the world, but I know that is the title you English really want. How is that expression, may the best man win. Do you know what Vogel means translated? I hope he is interested in flight like us too.

Must go soon, another rehearsal, the trio me, sis and the girl from the upstairs flat. She is very nice. A sweet pie but she can’t fly so goodbye for now, your friend

Henry’

TEDDY

(Begins to compose reply)

Really Henry girls; Messerschmitt, let me give you two words : Rolls - Royce

Distracted by door opening downstairs, Terence heard coming home from work, radio retuned from news to dance music, downstairs door opening

INGRID

Edward, tea.

Teddy closes letter, takes stamps and slides down banister downstairs

TEDDY

Good evening father. I saved you the stamps.

TERENCE

Thank you, son. The answer is still no.

INT. SCHOOL MUSIC ROOM, VIENNA - DAY

Ilse conducting ‘her’ trio very intensely

ILSE

No, Henryk, it is like this. (She plays Henryk’s piano part.) Now again, from the top, 1 and 2 and

The trio, Ilse, Henryk, GRETA play Der Hirt auf den Felsen over INTERCUT scene of Werner’s rail journey. he looks at landscape, reads a political pamphlet, falls asleep, train arriving in Vienna main station, checks his work contract, disembarks, at the control barrier; very severe checks on a family in front of and after him but he is saluted and waved through although name on his work contract is noted by police. He proceeds to clock on main concourse, very busy, high security around him. He waits…

INT. THE STERN’S ROOM ABOVE THE WORKSHOP - LATER THE SAME DAY

JOSEF

Henryk my son you may leave us

HENRYK

But, we, I

JOSEF

Thank you, Henryk.

He leaves. Begins practising scales on piano in workshop downstairs. His mother exits. Piano abruptly stops.

Ilse, what do you have to say for yourself?

I, your mother and I, view this matter very seriously. I am asking you if you have anything you wish to say, anything in mitigation?

ILSE

What am I on trial for? I am a musician. I'm sorry but music is my job not meeting Naz…people at railway stations.

JOSEF

You are, my dear, missing the point. As you well know. You are an intelligent girl, gifted even, your mother and I are not without ears, we are not without generosity, but we are not here to be taken advantage of.

ILSE

Taken advantage of. I don't know what you mean.

JOSEF

The point is you have let down the family, you have let your mother and I down.

ILSE

He is quite capable of making his own way from the station. Music comes first.

JOSEF

Family come first. I asked you to perform a simple task for me, a courtesy. You did not do as I asked. I am asking you what you have to say for yourself, young lady.

ILSE

Do you want me to apologise.

JOSEF

I want you to recognise on this occasion you have let your mother and I down. I want you to know, for your own future sake, the importance of courtesy.

ILSE

C - O - U - R - T - E - S - Y! I have a word for you, my dear old fashioned..

HELENE

(re-enters room on hearing ' old fashioned')

Ilse! Enough.

ILSE

I have a word for you my dear old fashioned father: W - A - R. Yes, and where will your courtesy be then?

JOSEF

There is not going to be a war. Where have you heard such things? There have been too many wars, there will not be another.

ILSE

There will be a war, I feel it: Germany and Austria against England and America.

JOSEF

Where have you heard such things?

HELENE

Answer your father.

At this point Henryk enters

ILSE

Henryk had a letter from his English pen pal. This boy is going to be a pilot, he said the British Empire are building a secret monoplane to stop Germany taking over the world, he said..

JOSEF

Ilse stop this. There is not going to be a war. I have been in a war. I know.

HELENE

Your father is right. All you know is music. And if you don’t stop, and apologise there will be no peace.

ILSE

I apologise. I know what you and Mother do for me. I do. Really I do.

JOSEF

Very well. We understand each other , all is well. You and Henryk may carry on with your music. Family, courtesy, music.

ILSE

In that order?

She leaves to go downstairs

JOSEF

And Ilse..

ILSE

Yes, father?

JOSEF

Be civil to Werner. I don’t know if he is in politics or not. It is not my - our - concern. He is young, he is here to make music, the same as you .

Ilse and Henryk go downstairs. Josef hugs Helene.

JOSEF

Everything will be alright.

HELENE

Promise?

Piano and clarinet rehearsal music starts from downstairs.

EXT. LEEDS ALLOTMENT - AFTERNOON

Teddy and his father working in the allotment, picking vegetables to take home for tea. They wheel tandem cycle home laden with vegetables. Ingrid waiting on doorstep. Just before they enter Terence speaks to Teddy.

TERENCE

If that is what you really want, I'll think about it.

INT. A LOCAL CINEMA IN LEEDS - EVENING

Terence and Teddy watching newsreel of aircraft speed competition, sound of aircraft to sound of trams. INTERCUT

INT. STERN WORKSHOP - MORNING

Werner, alone, is admiring the clarinet Josef is fitting, at sound of door opening he recovers the instrument.

WERNER

Good morning, Herr J …Oh

GRETA

Good morning, my name is Greta

WERNER

Werner Vogel. At your service.

GRETA

What are you looking at?

WERNER

Nothing. I mean, I'm looking at you.

GRETA

I've heard all about you.

WERNER

You've heard all about me?

GRETA

Don't worry. Good things, you were top of your class in Berlin. Tell me about Berlin.

WERNER

Berlin, what do you want to know? Tell me about Vienna.

GRETA

Clever you, changing the subject so the girl talks. Boys do that.

WERNER

You know a lot of boys?

GRETA

Tell me about Berlin.

WERNER

Berlin, Vienna, what's the big difference?

GRETA

I can show you. I can show you around Vienna.

WERNER

I'm here to work

GRETA

Do you know the English expression ' all work and no play make Werner a ….'

WERNER

I discontinued my English studies at school. It is not necessary to my work.

HENRYK (enters)

Good morning, I am Henryk. I am delighted I have my new spectacles. Look. I can sight read again.

He walks straight to piano and begins to play the piece he is rehearsing for the concert. He talks over the playing

Do you like Mendelsohn?

WERNER

I like, er, I like…

GRETA

What do you like, Werner?

JOSEF

Good morning, I am so pleased to see all - nearly all - the young people together.

Together-

GRETA] Good morning, Mr Stern

WERNER]Good morning, Herr Meister

JOSEF

Henryk, thank Herr Mendelsohn, that will be all .

HENRYK

Father, look my new glasses.

JOSEF

A time for work, a time for play, whichever way you look at it. Off you go young man, school. Greta would you excuse us? Werner and I have work to attend to.

GRETA

Remember, if you want to see Vienna..

JOSEF

Now, young Herr Vogel. Let us begin our work.

WERNER

Herr Meister Stern, Good morning. How is your daughter today?

JOSEF

My daughter is well. She has apologised for her oversight at the railway station. Not the best of starts I admit. That is behind us now. I have a special project for you. Shall we begin.

INT. HENRYK'S ROOM - LATER THE SAME DAY

He is reading aloud as he writes

'Dear Teddy

What a stink! Father asked my big sister Ilse to meet his new apprentice Werner Vogel at the railway station. He is mad at her because she didn't go. All she thinks of is music. We are practising every day for the big concert.

You're invited. Of course it would be a long journey. I have to imagine it in reverse. Leeds London Harwich through Holland across Germany Vienna. It is a journey I would love to make one day.

When you are a pilot I could come and see you in your Royal Air force uniform. I wish I could be a pilot but even with my new glasses I don't suppose it will ever happen. Perhaps one day you will take me up ..

INTERCUT to INT. TEDDY'S ROOM

Teddy continues reading Henryk's letter, sounds of Teddy's parents talking with animation downstairs is mixed with dance music from the radio.

TEDDY

..in a crate for a spin' - Good old, Henry! - 'I am sorry I have not been able to obtain the latest pictures of the international trains arriving into Vienna main station. I offered to go to meet Werner from the Berlin arrival instead of Ilse but Papa wouldn't let me. I hope my eyes continue to improve and I will be able to go again. I know they are not photos of trains but here are some pictures of my family and friends, here is our trio, Ilse, Greta and I. May be one day we will be on the BBC!

Your friend

Henry'

Girls! Ilse, Greta..

The conversation downstairs stops, radio retuned to BBC news. Call from downstairs

INGRID

Edward, teatime

Teddy considers adding the pictures of the girls to his gallery of trains, pilots, cricketers but then puts them back in envelope, tears off stamps, bounds downstairs into family dining room. Radio news continues.

TERENCE

Do we need to have this on?

INGRID

I want to know what is happening in the world.

Terence turns off radio

TERENCE

I want to know what's for tea

TEDDY

I want to know about the new aircraft you are working on.

INGRID

Edward, what has got into you. Behave.

TEDDY

And when it is operational I'm going to fly it. You promised.

INGRID

Terence?

TERENCE

What gave you that idea? Teddy, Edward, what gave you that idea?

TEDDY

Well, am I wrong?

There is no response. Teddy leaves the dining table, grabs his school bag and runs out. Ingrid stands to follow him, but Terence indicates to let him be.

INTERCUT

EXT. STREET OUTSIDE TERRACED HOUSE - DAY

Teddy runs along street, past factories, along railway embankment, Doppler sound of steam train passing with covered, possible military, wagons.

Teddy makes to wave but train is blacked out. He sits on embankment. He looks around then takes from his bag a bottle of beer, opens with a scout knife, and swigs. He thinks of throwing the empty bottle on the track but a friendly bobby passes.

BOBBY

Evening, son. Celebrating are we. Which birthday may I ask?

TEDDY

I'm old enough to be in the R A F, I'm old enough to drink beer, I'm old enough to

BOBBY

Right you are son, I'm old enough to have heard it all before. What are you doing out here? Any more tricks in that bag, bottle of bubbly for when Greta Garbo shows up. Speak up.

Bobby escorts Teddy home, bangs on door, he salutes Terence, Teddy goes inside and straight to his room.

INTERCUT

INT. FROM TEDDY’S ROOM TO TOP OF STAIRS - EVENING

A heated discussion can be heard from the sitting room below, the words become discernible as Teddy moves from his room to top of stairs

TERENCE

..We are not going to have wars in this house. You of all people should know that. He is old enough now to make his own decisions. I know he can be difficult at times, you do your very best for him. We have discussed it now. Please call him down.

INGRID

Edward. Your father would like to speak to you.

TERENCE

Son, how would you like to join the air cadets?

You must keep up your school work, mind, if you want to be a high flier in every sense of the word.

And Teddy, beer and aircraft don’t mix. Are you receiving me?

EXT. VIENNA MAIN STATION INTERNATIONAL ARRIVALS - DAY

Henryk is fumbling with his box camera, a policeman notices him, suspicious at first but noting Henry’s short sight he asks another policeman to hold the box camera and take a snap shot of policeman and Henryk in front of the steam train arriving from Berlin.

INTERCUT INT. HENRYK RETURNS ON THE TRAM TO

INT. WORKSHOP - DAY

ILSE

Henryk, where have you been?

He goes directly to piano. The camera is still in his rucksack. He takes out camera to get his music then puts camera back in pack, adjusts his spectacles and is ready.

GRETA

Can Werner stay in his workshop for our dress rehearsal?

ILSE

No, Greta, Werner cannot stay in my father's workshop at his moment. (Werner walks towards Greta) Musicians only. (Werner leaves) 1 - 2 - 3 and..

She conducts their central party piece from the clarinet. At certain moments she instructs:

more pianissimo, less staccato, lento..

During this piece INTERCUT EXT. 1 to Teddy's first parade as air cadet, INTERCUT EXT. 2 Werner and Greta at the Prater then back to the rehearsal. INT. Helene enters to put up some decorations, but does not interrupt music and is not noticed by Ilse. At the end Helene applauds.

HELENE

Bravo, bravo

ILSE

It still needs more work. One more time..

HELENE

It is perfect, darling. Unimprovable.

ILSE

No such word.

HELENE

It is Friday, time for dinner at the AUGE'S upstairs. Everyone invited. Now.

She gathers everyone together, Ilse leaves reluctantly, as they go upstairs Josef and Werner enter the workshop.

HELENE

Darling, everyone means everyone. It is Friday evening, Herr Auge will think it is rude.

JOSEF

We will be up very presently.

Josef and Werner alone in the workshop remove the cover from their work, the new clarinet. Werner examines the keys. He gives an approving whistle.

Josef places the clarinet in a case marked with the insignia of his business.

INT. JACOB AUGE'S FLAT AT TOP OF BUILDING - EVENING

JACOB

Welcome, welcome, welcome, Josef old friend, your lovely wife, the gifted Ilse, Mr Henryk - I am sure you are gifted too in your own way, young man, here we all our, my lovely wife, my guiding star..

MAGDA

Jacob!

JACOB

And who I may ask is this fine young gentleman?

JOSEF

Jacob, let me introduce my new master craftsman apprentice, Herr Vogel, from Berlin, Werner

JACOB

Ah, Berlin, yes, such a great metropolis, you are most welcome, young sir, I hope Vienna is not too, too..

ILSE

Provincial?

JACOB

Too, too, quiet for a young fellow from Berlin.

WERNER

Thank you, Herr Auge, Vienna is most agreeable, most charming.

GRETA

Come, Werner, you are so polite

JACOB

Charming, yes, a good description of our fine city, full of the charms of music, isn't that so Ilse

ILSE

Yes, not exactly on the same level as the great cities of London or

JACOB

London, what times we had there Josef old friend, I remember..

MAGDA

To the table everyone, welcome all, Greta, make sure our young guest is comfortable. Ilse sit next to me, tell me all about the great concert. I'm sure we can match anything London has to offer.

JACOB

And Josef, do you still keep up with our friends from London days?

JOSEF

I hope you are not implying my instruments are not as fine as those made in London.

JACOB

In London, we were like your young man Herr Vogel. Apprentices. In Vienna we are masters. Your instruments are the finest in the world

HENRYK

Your glasses are the finest in the world

JACOB

The least I could do, my boy

ILSE

No excuse for any mistakes in your sight reading now, dear Henryk.

JACOB

What a splendid young fellow he is becoming now, a credit to you, my dear Josef.

JOSEF

Indeed so. Not the most dextrous of chaps but there are so many ways of making your way in the world these days.

HELENE

Henryk, tell Herr Auge how your English is developing, he will be most interested.

JACOB

English, the language of Shakespeare, the 'sceptred isle..'

HENRYK

I write nearly everyday to my pen pal in England. I never need to use a dictionary now. English and music, of course, are my favourite subjects at school.

JACOB

Most interesting, well done young man, and where in London does your English friend reside?

HENRYK

Leeds.

JOSEF

Henryk..

HENRYK

North Leeds.

WERNER

(seated at the table next to Greta)

What will you be showing me next in your city?

GRETA

(Noticing his plate)

Don't you like Mother's delicacies, she will be most offended.

HENRYK

Delicious.

WERNER

I invite you to Berlin, little man, I'll show you..

ILSE

Are you calling my brother, little man?

WERNER

No offence.

ILSE

He is the second most important member of my trio.

GRETA

No offence.

ILSE

I hope I'm not interrupting you two, but Greta, I need to talk to Werner.

GRETA

What about?

ILSE

Music, silly, what else is there to talk about?

WERNER

I am at your service.

ILSE

So, what are you going to do at the concert?

GRETA

Leave Werner alone, he is a craftsman, not a musician.

ILSE

But he represents the great German tradition, all the way from Berlin, he isn't going to wriggle out of it that easily.

WERNER

Wriggle?

HENRYK

Wriggle out, evade, funk, shirk

WERNER

Shirk?

ILSE

The great German tradition. What is it to be, there is a slot in the programme after our trio.

WERNER

Of course, I would be honoured, the great German tradition. Wagner, Goethe, Schiller.

ILSE

So what is it to be, I hope you are not going to parrot a list. Let me have the opus numbers when you've narrowed your selection down. Perhaps you would like to give us a rendition of your beloved Wagner right now, a poem, a song, perhaps.

HENRYK

Oh, yes Werner, do.

JOSEF

Ilse

ILSE

Why not, it would be an honour Werner, wouldn't it.

GRETA

Ilse

ILSE

What is it to be? You don't want to let the fatherland down now do you?

WERNER

I would like to sing a song by Richard Wagner, no I would like to recite a poem by Goethe.

ILSE

Why are we waiting.

GRETA

Henryk, please, play us your latest piece on our piano.

JACOB

Yes, my boy, how is the sight reading now?

Henryk rescues the situation by playing a piano piece by Mendelssohn from sight at Herr Auge's piano. Applause, meal resumes.

HELENE

Ilse, what are you trying to do?

MAGDA

The young gentleman is probably a little shy. Here try some of these Viennese fancies I have baked myself.

WERNER

Thank you, no.

MAGDA

You must

GRETA

Mother! Never mind Werner, we can rehearse something ourselves for the concert. Father can we be excused?

They leave together. Werner pauses at the door.

GRETA

Come on Werner, we can look in father's study for some songs or poems we can rehearse together. There isn't a moment to lose.

INT. TEDDY'S ROOM - LATE AFTERNOON

Reflection in room mirror of Teddy changing his school cap for air cadet cap. Door open. News reel heard from downstairs, ring of bicycle bell outside, Terence enters downstairs.

INGRID

How was your day, darling?

TERENCE

Don't ask.

INGRID

You look tired.

TERENCE

You look worried. Shouldn't be listening to all this.

He retunes radio to test match summary.

Priorities.

INGRID

If you don't mind, I was listening to that. The political situation is very grave. Mr Chamberlain says so. I'm worried.

TERENCE

Your family will be fine, Hamburg isn't Bavaria, everything will be fine.

INGRID

How do you know, how can you say that. I would like us to go to Hamburg, see people,family. We could even have a cycling holiday, like we did before…

TERENCE

Out of the question. For now. After, later.

INGRID

It might be too late.

TERENCE

Why should it be too late?

INGRID

The things I hear on the news, postcards from Hamburg, between the lines, war in the air.

TERENCE

Everything will be fine.

INGRID

'Everything will be fine.' War, England and Germany, it happened before.

TERENCE

Which is why it won't happen again.

Teddy closes his door, voices downstairs continue, inaudibly but heated. Radio retuned back to news then back to music. Upstairs Teddy has retuned his crystal radio set to same music to keep the voices out. He opens an envelope, takes out letter from Henryk, a photo of Vienna falls out. He checks his air cadet uniform, turns off radio and goes downstairs, voices stop as he reaches door into dining room.

INT. JACOB AUGE'S FLAT - SAME EVENING AFTER THEIR FRIDAY MEAL.

Greta enters.

MAGDA

Where have you been?

GRETA

Reading Goethe.

JACOB

That's my girl.

MAGDA

Be careful with that Werner.

GRETA

Ilse was rude to him. He is our guest.

JACOB

That’s my girl.

MAGDA

Just be careful.

GRETA

Why?

MAGDA

He is older than you, he is from a different country.

GRETA

We speak the same language.

MAGDA

Words aren’t everything.

JACOB

Come, mother, they are both young, doing what young people do. Greta, my dear, what did you two decide on for the concert?

GRETA

A surprise.

MAGDA

I hope you are both right. I just feel he has..

JACOB AND GRETA]

What?

MAGDA

He has.. I feel he has an agenda

JACOB

It’s late.

GRETA

I’ll help clear away, big day tomorrow.

INT. WERNER’S ROOM - NIGHT

Werner restless, puts on light, he picks up a book of poetry briefly, then some leaflets he has picked up, one a craftsman trade union anti national socialist flyer, one advocating union of Austria and Germany. He rips up trade union flyer. Looks again at union leaflet. Then at the concert programme, his name inked in over the print.

INT. JOSEF’S WORKSHOP - THE NEXT DAY, EVENING

Decorations, Austrian flag, banner of craftsman’s guilds, candles, ‘happy birthday Ilse’..

JOSEF

Friends all it gives me such pleasure to welcome everyone of you here this evening. 9 November 1938, history in the making; it is the occasion of our beloved daughter’s 16th birthday – how time flies – so as music is the food of love, we have everything on offer this special evening: love, food, music. My lovely wife Helene and our close friend Magda have prepared the very best of Viennese delights for your delectation, this will be followed by the very best music our..

GRETA

And words.

Josef checks his programme where Werner has been inked in to recite.

MAGDA

Greta dearest, don't interrupt our host

JOSEF

..indeed the very best words and music our culture, and our cultured young people offer. I am so proud..

HELENE

Josef, food, time to serve our guests, you can't eat culture.

JOSEF

How right you are, my dear, priorities. Friends please, and then music.

Wonderful food is laid out at bedecked tables

JACOB

Ladies you have done us proud.

GRETA

Werner, are you ready?

WERNER

I was up all night.

GRETA

Hero.

ILSE

Greta, you need to focus.

GRETA

I am.

ILSE

It's nearly time, band meeting. Henryk.

HELENE

It's time, Josef. Presentation. And don't forget to mention your apprentice, he might not be everyone's cup of tea but he played his part.

JOSEF

Ladies and Gentlemen, your attention please. Once again I thank the ladies for making such a splendid occasion possible. Now, music. We are all so proud of our resident trio, Greta, Henryk - I'm sorry who is the third - yes, of course, Ilse, all blessed with the gift of music..

JACOB

Music, the blessing of our people

JOSEF

..And on the occasion of our daughter's birthday, my wife and I wish to present her with the gift of this musical instrument. I always say I can't make music but in this way I can. A labour of love is no labour.

I am honoured too to mention the most recent addition to our workshop, should I say to our family, Herr Werner, who has played his part in the making of this instrument. The finest our company has to offer to the finest of our family, ladies and gentleman, happy birthday, Ilse.

Henryk plays 'happy birthday' at the piano as Josef presents Ilse with the new clarinet.

ILSE

Father, thank you, thank you, it is so beautiful, thank you, I am so happy.

JOSEF

The moment of truth. Ladies and Gentlemen the Ilse Stern trio now perform for your pleasure ' Der Hirt auf dem Felsen.'

Ilse counts them in, they play. Ilse clarinet, Henryk at the piano, Greta sings. Applause.

ILSE

Thank you all, thank you father, I'll never forget it.

JOSEF

Thank you. And now a solo piece by my favourite son, Henryk, featuring Herr Auge's glasses.

As Henryk plays Ilse circulates thanking everyone

ILSE

Werner, I know you too played your part in making this fine instrument and you kept my father company on late nights in the workshop.

Thank you.

WERNER

I am honoured to be of assistance.

ILSE

And what piece have you chosen?

GRETA

We chose it together.

WERNER

You could say a joint German - Austrian choice, although the poet is of course German.

ILSE

I look forward to it.

Applause for Henryk

JOSEF

And now, as they say, a bombe surprise. My wife and Greta in Delibes accompanied by the maestro again at the piano, Henryk.

Henryk sight reads.

JOSEF

All made possible by your excellent work, friend Jacob. Henryk is so pleased.

JACOB

Delighted to be of service. A lovely evening, truly international, the best of all worlds.

MAGDA

Bright music in dark times.

JOSEF

Dark times, my dear Magda? Not this evening, look around you.

Applause

JOSEF

Dear friends, women, wine, song, the best of all worlds, all countries. Before this lovely evening comes to a close..

GRETA

Herr Stern, do not forget Herr Vogel’s addition to the programme.

MAGDA

Greta

JOSEF

.. a toast, to music, to Ilse, to Austria, to Europe, peace and fellowship.

The toast is repeated

JOSEF

Yes, and before our memorable evening becomes just that, a memory, we have a late addition to our programme but continuing our international theme, I give you Herr Werner Vogel.

Werner steps forward. Applause. Then as he appears to be about to begin he freezes.

JOSEF

What do you have for us, young man.

GRETA

The Soul of Man is Water by JW Goethe.

Jacob prompts him with first line, as soon as Werner continues a brick is hurled through the window. There is shock. Werner for a second is about to continue but there is a volley of missiles through all the front windows.

WERNER

Down, everyone down.

JACOB

So much for your Goethe.

Werner protects Greta, Josef recovers and gathers the young people, Jacob leads Helene and Magda under the food table as glass shatters, a mob enter, Josef and Jacob attempt to lead the group upstairs, at door Werner hesitates.

EXT. NEWSREEL OF KRISTALLNACHT INTERCUT STREET SCENE OUTSIDE THE STERN - AUGE FLAT / WORKSHOP - NIGHT

TEDDY V.O (reads aloud a letter from Henryk)

'I know we boys have to be brave but I am not ashamed to tell you how totally, totally scary it was. How can people be like that, they were everywhere, in the street, in the square, I thought we were going to die, there were no individuals, everyone had become one mob, a hydra, they were shouting 'Juden, Juden' like we weren't individuals, but a group to hunt like, like foxes. I'd never even heard the word 'Juden ' before. Papa was so brave, and Herr Auge, protecting us all. Yes, we are all safe, although Werner, father's apprentice from Germany has disappeared. I know it isn't a nice thing to say but I never really did like him. He never actually said that much but I didn't even like his silence. Silence! The noise of the mob was overwhelming.

INT. WORKSHOP - MORNING

After Kristallnacht, first light

Josef and Jacob are checking the workshop. ' Juden aus' slogans in mirror writing across what is left OF the windows, smashed signs for the workshop musical instrument / optician businesses. On the floor among the shards Josef finds Henryk's glasses with broken lenses, then the destroyed clarinet.

TEDDY (continues reading Henryk's words)

' Of course they are cowards, mobs are made up of cowards, we are good people, no one would dare to approach us individually, we are good citizens, artisans of Vienna, why has this happened to us, there is no reason. We are good people, musicians, workers, we have never, would never harm a soul, we don't even think harmful thoughts, we were playing Schubert, Mendelsohn, reading Goethe when they attacked us. We are lucky to be together, alive, though living upstairs all in one room, unable to go out, call that life…?'

Teddy folds up letter puts it in top pocket of his air cadet uniform, He and Terence cycle to Leeds RAF recruiting office

RAF OFFICER

Why do you want to join the RAF?

INT. WORKSHOP - NEXT DAY

Josef and Jacob sweeping up

JOSEF

No, I don’t know where he is. In the confusion and chaos we managed to get the women and children upstairs. We haven’t seen or heard from Werner since.

JACOB

He will be alright, he’s German.

JOSEF

He’s a young man alone in a strange city.

JACOB

Maybe it isn’t so strange to him anymore.

JOSEF

Meaning?

JACOB

We’ve done all we can here for now, let’s go upstairs, we need to have a meeting.

JOSEF

(He finds leaflets among the rubble on the workshop floor.)

Talk, talk, where does that get anyone.

JACOB

You, we, are all in a state of shock. We are musicians, music makers, craftspeople, something has happened that is beyond our understanding. But we can’t continue to live in one room forever. We must decide what to do.

JOSEF

What can we do in the face of a mob?

JACOB

That isn't you talking, the real you. I know.

JOSEF

I don't know whether to laugh or cry, us playing German music and poetry as they smash our windows.

You are right, we must believe in Beethoven and Goethe, the higher truth.

JACOB

Good old, Josef, onwards and upwards.

They climb the stairs to top flat where all family is living in makeshift quarters, washing on lines, toilet buckets, Josef hugs traumatised Henryk and Ilse and Helene, Jacob hugs Greta and Magda.

JOSEF

Before we decide on what we are going to do we are going to have a song.

HELENE

You have decided we are going to have a song.

JOSEF

Henryk, my man, what do you have for us?

HENRYK

My piano playing nearly killed us. Besides the glasses Herr Auge made for me are lost.

JOSEF

Henryk, my man, what do you have for us. You can play by heart.

He goes to piano, he begins to play Schubert ' So let me appear.' Some of the notes on the piano are missing. Greta joins in singing.

JOSEF

Thank you. I now declare this meeting open. Options?

HELENE AND MAGDA

We leave.

JACOB

We stay. I fought in the last war, we must stand up to bullies, culture must rule the mob.

MAGDA

Fine words, look where it has led us.

JOSEF

We are not here because of us, we are here because of others.

GRETA

Where is Werner?

JOSEF

We have to decide, our two families what to do, our circumstances are different to Werner's.

GRETA

Why?

MAGDA

Greta.

ILSE

What choices are open to us? We are musicians.

HELENE

We must take control now of what we can. I have heard people, people like us, leaving, leave while we can, with whatever we can. I have heard of people leaving with nothing.

MAGDA

What have you heard, specifics?

HELENE

Palestine, Shanghai, Brooklyn, Oslo, Stockholm

HENRYK

Leeds

ILSE

London

JOSEF

That's enough, we must be brave, we must be practical.

HELENE

We must leave

JACOB

We must stay. This is our country.

HELENE

We are not leaving our country, it is leaving us. We have already stayed too long. We should have seen this coming. Now look at us. Ilse where are you going?

ILSE

Air. Life. I need to breathe, play.

HELENE

Child, it is not safe. No one can go out.

ILSE

We must continue, music must continue. Perhaps one day we can go to London. For now we are Viennese.

JOSEF

When is your audition?

ILSE

Does it still make a difference?

JOSEF

Even more.

ILSE

I have nothing to wear, nothing to play..

JOSEF

Brahms

JACOB

Mendelsohn

HENRYK

Berg

ILSE

The clarinet, smashed, my spirit with it

JOSEF

I'll fix it. Them.

INT. VIENNA SCHOOL OF MUSIC - DAY

PRINCIPAL

No, you can’t play that. Mendelssohn is not on our syllabus.

ILSE

You asked me to prepare my favourite piece.

PRINCIPAL

Everything has changed. You will have to sight read. Brahms.

Please begin.

ILSE

Begins to play but suddenly freezes. Silence. Tries to start again. Door opens, aide enters with papers, principal looks at them, then waves hand to stop Ilse.

PRINCIPAL

Thank you, that will be all.

ILSE

What is wrong with my playing?

PRINCIPAL

There is nothing wrong with your playing.

She leaves clarinet, goes downstairs into foyer of academy. Henryk is waiting for her.

HENRYK

Father asked me to walk you home.

ILSE

Where is father?

HENRYK

I heard him talking to mother.

ILSE

What about?

HENRYK

Places.

ILSE

London?

HENRYK

He asked me to escort you home, and post these letters on the way. Leeds, London, Oslo, New York. I bought the stamps with my pocket money. I usually just buy my stamps for Leeds, father asked me specially.

They walk back through the streets. There is an increased military / police presence. As they enter their own district there is a police check.

OFFICER

Papers.

Checks Ilse's music case which has Josef's workshop sign. There is music and metronome in the case.

What is this, some kind of weapon, a code?

And you, what have you there, international letters, Austria and Germany not good enough for you?

This is the last time. I don't want to see you out again without your designated insignia.

ILSE

What regulations, officer? And did you catch the vandals who smashed our windows?

EXT. LEEDS ALLOTMENT - DAY
Terence picking veg from veg patch next to half finished air raid shelter he is making. Cycles home with veg for dinner. Three letters on the table, one with stamps from Vienna for Teddy, one marked 'Home Office' for Ingrid, two official R A F : one for Teddy, one for Terence. Terence opens his letter, type reads:

' .. too old to be considered for active service, however your expertise as a draughtsman may be of interest to the Air Ministry…'

He picks up letter addressed to Teddy, sees it has already been opened. Teddy enters

TERENCE

Where have you been?

TEDDY

Out

TERENCE

Your mother was worried about you.

What does your letter say?

TEDDY

What does yours?

TERENCE

Too old

TEDDY

Too young..

INGRID

Thank God

TEDDY

..to be a fighter pilot. I'm to report for radio operator training.

Mother, what does your letter say? It looks official.

INGRID

I prayed there would never be another war. If there was it would pass over us. Now we are flying right into it.

INT. WORKSHOP - DAY, VERY EARLY MORNING

Workshop lit by candles, one lamp, passing tram lights

Josef trying to improve the clarinet, Jacob trying to make Henryk new glasses.

Ilse enters, they are too tired and intent on their work in the low light to notice.

ILSE

Dear Father, that won't be necessary anymore. No more music. We are entering a world without music.

JOSEF

I don't understand. There is no world without music, impossible. Come on, off to school with you.

Henryk and Greta have entered

HENRYK

There is no school.

JOSEF

Where is Werner?

GRETA

There is no Werner. Not the one we knew.

JOSEF

He works for me. He is only in Vienna because of me, us.

JACOB

To use a carpenter's metaphor, old friend, you may find the tables have turned.

JOSEF

I must go out.

ILSE

What is the point?

Helene and Magda enter with a basket.

HELENE

Josef, you must eat, you must sleep.

Greta looks in the meagre basket and offers the contents, two bread rolls to Josef and Jacob.

Josef and Jacob about to leave by the front door.

HELENE

Where are you going?

JOSEF

Wherever we go I promise we will all go together.

EXT. CENTRAL VIENNA - DAY / EVENING

Josef and Jacob are on separate trams in Vienna diplomatic district. They queue by various embassy doors, leave, go to another embassy, queue, leave, as darkness falls, they meet and silently take the tram back. INTERCUT

HENRYK

(Reading V.O)

'..it seems a while since I heard from you. I bet you've met a girl and have forgotten all about me. I have more time to write now since school has been closed to us. I never thought I would say this but I miss school, putting on my uniform, riding the tram every day, learning your language, music lessons, tram home for tea, well, kaffee and kuche as we say here. Actually, we do have a new uniform of sorts now, I wear it whenever I do go out. Mother and Father and everyone are so brave, the beastly regulations make life very difficult for them. Father and his old friend - funny how friends always have the adjective 'old' in front of them, we are old friends now, Teddy. Of course I'll look you up when we are in England, London or Leeds. We are fortunate with our contacts, your family in Leeds, my father's business people in London, I know we will come one day. Father and his old friend Jacob are out all day trying for our exit visas. I would love to really meet you, old friend, you can teach me cricket, I want to be a real English gentleman, give up my seat to ladies on double decker buses..

Jacob and Josef standing exhausted on very crowded tram INTERCUT

EXT. LEEDS TRAM - DAY / EVENING

Teddy in R A F uniform reading Henryk’s letter on Leeds tram…

Do you like England, I don’t like Vienna anymore, there is no music and some bullies broke my glasses which Herr Auge made for me. Talk about seeing the world in a different way! May be you will be right, girls are more interesting than trains..’

Teddy alights from tram, continues reading by gaslight. CYNTHIA, heavily made up, old beyond her years, alights from tram arriving opposite.

CYNTH

Love letters! A rival! What’s her name?

TEDDY

Henryk

CYNTH

And what is Henryk writing to you about?

TEDDY

Bullies

CYNTH

I hope you are going to sort these bullies out.

TEDDY

You’ve been watching too many films.

CYNTH

I’m just waiting for the right one.

They enter cinema, Cynth and Teddy snogging through newsreel (newsreel refers to parliamentary debate House of Commons, London 21 Nov 1938)

INT. ROOM ABOVE WORKSHOP - EARLY MORNING

HELENE

Darling, stay home today, give it a rest.

JOSEF

I can't rest until..

HELENE

Until what?

JOSEF

Until we are all safe, all of us.

Banging on workshop door below

Josef and Jacob go down, Werner and police at door.

JOSEF

Werner. Are you in trouble with the police? Officers I can vouch for him. Werner, we can fix the instrument, no need to worry

POLICE OFFICER1

What instrument?

POLICE OFFICER2

You and members of your family have been out to Embassies of foreign powers without insignia.

Here are 7 insignia. This is your final warning. You are advised to comply with all regulations. Totally. For your own safety.

Josef and Jacob return upstairs

HELENE

Who was that?

JACOB

Herr Vogel, he’s in trouble with the police.

MAGDA

What is happening, what will happen to us?

JOSEF

I will keep trying. There are always options.

HELENE

I have heard of families leaving down the Danube to Palestine, I have heard of …

JOSEF

There are always options.

HELENE

Darling, don’t go out again.

JACOB

I will go with you.

JOSEF

No, today you stay with the families. I will keep trying. We will all leave together if Vienna no longer wants us.

EXT. TRAM CENTRAL VIENNA - DAY

Josef with star insignia riding the trams on further efforts to secure exit visas from embassies. Last call of day at Vienna district police. Josef enters office, bureaucrats with stamps, supervised by their junior manager, Werner. Josef waiting in overcrowded ante room. Werner sees Josef but ignores him. Josef sees Werner and goes towards him but way blocked by others who think he is queue jumping and officers escort him out. Josef back on street steadies himself against a wall covered in political slogans. Tram home in darkness. Back to flat, Ilse has cooked a soup. There isn't enough to go round, she offers some to Josef.

JOSEF

Music and cooking, quite the young lady now. It looks lovely but I've already eaten. Sure Henryk can manage some more.

Helene looks at him, he shakes his head

JOSEF

Seems no one wants us.

HELENE

There might be just one chance, for the young ones

JOSEF

We all go or we all stay.

HELENE

I have heard of a group in England called..

INT. LEEDS ENGINEERING WORKS TEST ROOM - DAY

Roar of aero engine, Terence with clipboard surrounded by R A F / air ministry officials, they nod to Terence approvingly. Terence leaves work and cycles home past airfield where Teddy was first spotting planes, past the allotment with air raid shelter, home for dinner with fresh veg.

As he cycles and arrives home V.O

Ingrid reading from official letter dated December 1938 over dinner

'..the Religious Society of Friends and other groups on receipt of the appropriate bond families who wish to receive children from the distressed areas should make themselves known to the local committee..'

As Terence and Ingrid on tram to Leeds, in local committee office, handing over deposit, forms stamped by official, they are having tea in Lyons café Leeds

INGRID

£50 deposit, tea at the best café in Leeds, perhaps you should tell me where the money is coming from.

TERENCE

Careless talk costs lives.

INGRID

Well. At least we may be saving some.

TERENCE

What does 'Kind' mean?

INGRID

In German, child, in English, kind. In human, doing the right thing.

TERENCE

Does Teddy know?

INGRID

I'll write to him at his unit, if someone will tell me where it is.

TERENCE

Chocks away, welcome to the war effort.

INGRID

I don't agree with war.

TERENCE

Neither do I. Sometimes you don't do what you want, you do..

INGRID AND TERENCE (Together)

..what is right.

INT.FLAT ABOVE WORKSHOP VIENNA - NIGHT, CANDLE LIGHT

JACOB

Sometimes you are called upon not to do what you want but what is right.

HELENE

I am a mother. I am deliberately breaking up my family, sending my children to strange lands..

JACOB

Safe lands

ILSE

England

HELENE

..strange lands, into the arms of strangers,

MAGDA

Open arms or clenched fists, do we have a choice?

JACOB

Josef, old friend, your silence is deafening. There is no choice, all the doors you tried to open are closed except this one. It is the right thing to do.

JOSEF

Ilse, can you take responsibility, when the train leaves the station, my responsibilities pass to you. For now, while you are away.

ILSE

I know you will follow. I will do my best.

JOSEF

Let us go over the plans once more. Ilse, check your papers and Henryk's and Greta's. Mother will give you a food basket at the station for your journey.

ILSE

What about you, what food do you have?

HELENE

We will be fine. We have each other. You will have Henryk. The family is still together. Rest now, then be ready with one suitcase each, your job is to orchestrate the others.

ILSE

Will you follow us to England? Promise?

EXT. TRAM THROUGH VIENNA - THE FOLLOWING DAY

All the family on tram to Vienna main station. Henryk ill, can hardly stand. He rubs his eyes and drops his glasses, tram too crowded for him to retrieve them.

HELENE

Henryk, I thought you would be looking forward to an international train ride, you will be able to see the places your father visited, to see Edward

At station very crowded, chaotic, high police presence.

JOSEF

Stay together, stay close.

JACOB

Henryk, where are your glasses?

At station Josef leads family to departure area, police checks, Josef sees one of the check lines is being controlled by Werner. He tries to switch lines but is pushed back. Eventually they reach barrier.

OFFICER

How many of you travelling?

JOSEF

3

OFFICER

Papers.

JOSEF

They have already been checked. Please, we need to go forward, my son is..

OFFICER

Papers. Final check here. If all in order those travelling proceed forward, those remaining are to return to processing area.

GESTAPO

What is the delay here?

Papers double checked

GESTAPO

You (Ilse) and you (Greta) go.

JOSEF

Officer…

OFFICER

I would advise you not to draw attention to yourself.

GESTAPO

This child (Henryk)is too sick to travel, the health certificate is not valid. You (Ilse)and you (Greta), proceed now.

Officer pulls Ilse and Greta away from Helene and Magda

HELENE

Remember what I told you. Be the best of us.

ILSE

Promise you will follow. Mother, Father, promise.

They are pulled apart. Ilse and Greta are engulfed by crowd escorted by armed police to very crowded train, the procession of children disappear into the steam in one direction, Josef, Jacob, Henryk, Helene, Magda escorted back to holding area in opposite direction. Official gives them more papers.

OFFICIAL

Nobody wants you.

HELENE

My children…

OFFICIAL

There will be another train along shortly for you I expect, and unlike the English, the Reichbahn will give you a free passage. Take these papers, go home.

HELENE (to officials)

You have destroyed my home, you should be ashamed.

JOSEF

Come, darling

HELENE

Where, what for, our children separated, we live in one room with no food.

JACOB

Magda, take Helene and Henryk home on the tram. Josef and I will walk.

INT. TRAIN CROSSING BORDER INTO GERMANY - NIGHT

Gestapo patrol inside the overcrowded train. Many children asleep, some crying, Ilse sings, shares the food from the basket, Greta in a state of shock. Day break at Dutch border. Nazi officials leave. Train crosses into Holland, food is passed into the train. Ilse sings, Greta, mentors and some older children join in.

GRETA

The sea, I have never seen the sea before.

ILSE

If only our parents and Henryk were here, we could pretend we were on holiday.

GRETA

We are too old for pretending, for games.

What do you think English people will be like?

ILSE

I expect they will be just like us.

GRETA

Do you think they will like us? Do you think they will like our music?

ILSE

I heard of some concerts they have every summer. Promenades. Everyone likes music.

GRETA

Why did we have to leave Vienna if everyone likes music. We play music.

ILSE

I am never going to play music again, not until we are all together again. Then we will give a promenade concert of our own. The Ilse Stern Trio at the Royal Albert Hall.

GRETA

The Auge Stern duo

ILSE

We will be together again. All of us.

GRETA

Promise?

EXT. KINGS CROSS STATION - DAY

Steam train arrives at Kings Cross, Terence and Ingrid take underground to Liverpool Street

TERENCE

Well, you can speak German again. Old girl. (Looks at official letter) Ilse.

INGRID

Elsie

At Liverpool Street they join the welcome committee

WELCOME COMMITTEE OFFICIAL

Mr and Mrs Lambert. We are expecting the arrival in 30 minutes. Here is the welcome package for the children, what to expect, it'll be a shock for them, rain, fish and chips..

INGRID

People being friendly

OFFICIAL

Quite. Just one point. Your Ilse..

INGRID

Elsie

OFFICIAL

..and her friend Greta have already been separated from their families. It will be an additional shock for them to be separated from each other.

TERENCE

If it is a question of money we can put up a bond for them both.

OFFICIAL

That needed to be taken care of in advance. Home Office regulation. Greta Auge will be lodged with a colleague of her father's, an optician, in the West Country. All will be well when they are settled. Fortunately they are both high fliers…

TERENCE

That would suit Teddy down to the ground..

INGRID

Edward is for, with, Cynthia

OFFICIAL

High fliers, Ilse – Elsie – and Greta, excelled at school in music and English. That will be a huge advantage. Most of the poor mites are going to struggle with the language on top of everything else.

If you would like to join the other reception families, tea and sandwiches are available. And may I thank you on behalf of the Committee for what you are doing.

INGRID

Thank you

They join group on the station, a (Quaker) couple hand them tea

Mrs TREGOWAN

Where are you from?

INGRID

Hamburg

TERENCE

We're from Leeds

Mr TREGOWAN

That will be an advantage

TERENCE

Being from Leeds

Mrs TREGOWAN

It is good to know we can all make a difference in the world.

Mr TREGOWAN

Force isn't everything

Mrs TREGOWAN

Do you have children of your own?

TERENCE

Our son is in the R A F

INGRID

How do you think the Nazis can be stopped?

Mrs TREGOWAN

Kindness. Silence. Bearing witness.

INGRID

Who is your 'kind'?

Mr TREGOWAN

Her name is Greta Auge. Yours?

INGRID

Elsie Stern. Very musical we are told.

Mrs TREGOWAN

So is ours. Perhaps we can compare notes, keep in touch.

Whistle of steam train, doors open, children on the platform, committee leaders escort them to the reception area, Ilse and Greta hold hands in the crowd, their numbered labels are checked they are led to the holding area.

INGRID

My name is Ingrid Lambert. It is an honour to meet you, to be of service.

TERENCE

Mr Lambert. Terence.

ILSE

I am Ilse Stern. This is Greta Auge.

INGRID

Welcome to England, we hope you will be happy here.

GRETA

When will our families be coming, it's cold, I'm hungry.

ILSE

Greta, these people are here to help us.

Mr TEGOWAN

Greta. We are the Tregowans.

Welcome. Come with us. You are safe now.

GRETA

Why, were to?

ILSE

My parents told us to stay together.

TERENCE

For now we are your parents. In loco parentis.

ILSE

My parents told us to stay together. I am to act as Greta's guardian until our families arrive.

Mrs TREGOWAN

We will look after you. It is for the best. Come along.

COMMITTEE LEADER

The arrangements have been made in your interest. Ilse go with Mr and Mrs Lambert, Greta with your new family. They are right, it is for the best, they will look after you.

ILSE

We have already been separated from our families. And now this. It isn't fair.

COMMITTEE LEADER

You are safe now. These arrangements have been made. Go with your new families. One more train journey. Each. All will be well.

GRETA (breaks into tears, in German)

It is too much. We have done nothing wrong.

INGRID (in German)

All will be well. This is what you must do now. And I will not talk German again. Ilse, Greta, you are both safe here. Do as you are told.

TERENCE

You can write to each other, and see each other soon.

ILSE

Promise, we will see each other and our families soon.

TERENCE

You will see each other soon.

Ilse and Greta are separated, they leave on different trains with their 'parents.'

EXT. TRAIN NORTH - SAME DAY

TERENCE

We hear you are very musical.

INGRID

We look forward to welcoming you into our home.

TERENCE

We have our own allotment. Lots of fresh vegetables. For tea.

Ingrid translates allotment thinking Ilse doesn't understand

ILSE

You don't need to do that. I understand the word. I don't know what an allotment is but I understand the word. I am sure my mother will be most grateful I am going to a house where there are fresh vegetables for tea.

EXT. GRETA'S TRAIN JOURNEY - SAME DAY

She is silent and stares out at her own reflection in the train window.

INT. UPSTAIRS ROOM IN FLAT ABOVE VIENNA WORKSHOP - DAY

Nothing to eat, Henryk weak

JOSEF

Henryk, would you be so kind as to play us something on Herr Auge's piano?

HELENE

The boy is not well.

Henryk crosses room to piano and begins to play Beethoven sonata 'fur Elise', there are notes missing on the keyboard, he comes to a halt , silence.

EXT. A VIEW OF INDUSTRIAL LEEDS - DAY

TEDDY V.O.

My dear Henryk, I was so pleased to hear from you. Please forgive my what you might call radio silence for a while in not writing back to you. I suppose things have moved on. There are still as always aeroplanes, new ones, can't say any more old boy but I will let you in on a secret, a girl. Here name is Cynthia. No, not really a secret, I am very proud of her. I met her at Mecca. When I am on leave and you come on the train to Leeds I'll take you there. Promise. Perhaps you are more interested in girls than trains and planes too now. It happens to us all..

INTERCUT

INT. RAF AERODROME - EARLY MORNING

Teddy writing from his bunk

I've been busy at training school and am about to pass out..'

INTERCUT

INT. VIENNA FLAT - DAY

HENRYK (Writing)

He tells me he is away from home at the Royal Air Force . I am so pleased to hear from him. I have never met him but he seems almost family, especially now…

INTERCUT

INT. UPSTAIRS IN THE LEEDS TERRACED HOUSE - EVENING

Ilse reading his letter in Teddy's old room, the model aircraft still suspended from the ceiling

HENRYK (Continued, V.O)

'…Father and Herr Auge no longer ride the trams everyday visiting the Embassies, we don't go out very much, we will stay here for the time being. Tell me your impressions of the city…'

Ilse goes to the window, view of factories and smoke, nightfall, falls into fitful sleep, images of Vienna, fragments of music from the concert, woken by factory hooter, sees pictures of aircraft and trains, envelopes with Henryk's handwriting..

ILSE (jolts awake)

Henryk? Mutti, Papa?

INGRID

(from downstairs)

Elsie, breakfast

In front room, pictures of Teddy's engagement to Cynth, wedding photo of Ingrid and Terence

ILSE

My name is Ilse

INGRID

I know, love. Elsie is Yorkshire for Ilse.

ILSE

Where is your son?

INGRID

Royal Air Force

And do you want to know about the girl in the photo too?

ILSE

And your husband?

INGRID

Factory. Draughtsman. Yes, that's all I know too.

ILSE

Your accent, where are you really from?

INGRID

Leeds

ILSE

Like me. I mean really?

INGRID

Leeds. Really. Hamburg

ILSE

Why did you come here? Are Teddy and Henryk pen pals by coincidence?

INGRID

Questions! A healthy curiosity. I know. It was strange too for me at first.

ILSE

What is this?

INGRID

Bacon and egg

ILSE

Aren't you having any?

INGRID

Your journey was longer than mine. Treat. Welcome to Leeds. Love.

INT. FACTORY FLOOR LEEDS - NIGHT
Terence on factory floor with plans, Spitfire prototypes taking shape

TERENCE

Soon be your time, beauty. Pity, you weren't ready earlier.

Factory hooter, he cycles home very early morning

EXT. VIENNA APARTMENT - EARLY MORNING

An exhausted Josef crumples another rejection letter from embassy, he is about to put on hat, armband etc. to go out again but sits down at old piano stool writes a few words in a notebook, stops, about to cry.

HENRYK Papa?

INT. LEEDS PARISH CHURCH - DAY

A schools choir concert, Ilse doesn't know the words of hymns, choir accompanied by 'scratch' orchestra. An English high tea served in church hall after concert.

HEAD GIRL, MAVIS

Tuck in, old girl

ILSE

(looking at pork pies etc)

What are they?

After concert Ilse waiting with other girls for school bus, some girls have picked up on her slight accent.

1

Vould you like a sandvich?

2

Vhy not

HEAD GIRL

Knock it off, little minds.

INT. LEEDS SCHOOL, HEAD MISTRESS OFFICE - DAY

HEADMISTRESS (To Ingrid)

I had hoped your husband would be here too but I understand he is very busy. Air Ministry isn't it?

Yes, Elsie, although some of the girls did call her The German Girl on her first day, partly on account of her V and W pronunciation, but that has now ceased. Her English is quite remarkable. In fact all things considered she is a remarkable young lady. I gather she was the leader of a musical trio at home.

INGRID

This is her home.

HEADMISTRESS

I understand. What contact does she have with her real family?

INGRID

Letters from parents, brother Henryk – we corresponded with Henryk before, before…. Her sister was transferred to the West Country on arrival but I hope she will visit shortly. Home from home. Is there a problem?

HEADMISTRESS

As headmistress I would hardly describe it as a problem.

INGRID

I thought she was doing so well.

HEADMISTRESS

She is.

INGRID

I am not following you.

HEADMISTRESS

Follow. Sorry, my mistake, headmistress habit. There is no problem. Remarkable.

INGRID

I don't follow you.

HEADMISTRESS

Some of the girls have complained she is too clever.

EXT. LAMBERT'S HOUSE - DAY

Ilse cycles back from allotment with fresh veg & some wild flowers, enters begins cooking, reads a Red Cross letter, smiles to herself.

ILSE

Promise

Ingrid enters, notices flowers are really weeds, about to remove them from milk bottle vase but leaves them, they are working together in the kitchen.

INGRID

Tea break

ILSE

Isn't a tea break when we have a break from tea?

They sit at table, Ilse re-reads her Red Cross letter, Ingrid has letter from Teddy.

INGRID

You first

ILSE

After you

INGRID

You have delightful manners, which school did you learn those in, Leeds or Vienna. How are things at home? Really.

ILSE

You are still young enough for both your parents to be alive

INGRID

..charmed I’m sure..

ILSE

Where are they?

INGRID

Tell me about your parents?

ILSE

Tell me about yours.

INGRID

Are you interested in politics?

ILSE

Politics doesn’t concern me.

INGRID

Hamburg SPD. Socialist Party Deutschland. Our journey was from Hamburg to Bradford. 1934.

ILSE

You and your parents. A choice.

INGRID

I don't think we would choose the word choice.

I travelled from Bradford to Leeds. Single. I got on Terence's tandem at a Labour party cycling club. Mother and Father went on to USA. Business. Back to you.

ILSE

Father has such a stiff upper lip, but then he is a carpenter, well an instrument maker to be accurate.

He has been to every Embassy in the diplomatic district. I am sure they will soon be here.

INGRID

And your little brother.

ILSE

Not so little now. I hope he can help father. Mr Auge made him some new spectacles but the bullies smashed them. His health is fragile, that's why…that's why

INGRID

You are here and he isn't.

ILSE

Except in spirit. And letters of course.

INGRID

For now. That's life, luck versus chance. He will be here. Greta can come up from down south and..

ILSE

We proudly present The Ilse - Elsie - stern Trio in a performance of Elgar, Vaughn Williams and … sorry, my manners, what is in your letter. You've managed to tell me what isn't in it.

INGRID

Can't tell you, enemy alien. Come on, tea.

ILSE

We've just had tea.

INGRID

I mean tea. Father, Terence, will be home any minute. Put the radio on. No, not news, music.

Terence enters

TERENCE

What's for tea. (Sees Red Cross letter) what is the news of your family. How is school?

ILSE

They have asked me to play clarinet in a school concert. I must write back to Papa after dinner. I wish I could have brought his best clarinet with me from the workshop but..

INT. FRIENDS MEETING HOUSE - DAY

A simple room with aspect overlooking sea. Greta sits in silence with her Quaker 'family', silence interrupted ..INTERCUT..

EXT. VIENNA WORKSHOP - DAWN

..by police banging on door of Josef's workshop

JOSEF

Can I help you Gentlemen?

INT. LEEDS HOUSE - DAY

During meal prepared from allotment veg by Ingrid and Ilse, Terence unexpectedly comes home, leaves tandem on ground outside house, walks straight in and turns on RADIO:

'We interrupt this broadcast for a special announcement from the prime minister..

'consequently this country is at war with Germany..'

INGRID

Eat your greens,love

INT.RAF AERODROME - DAY

ADJUTANT

Letter, Lambert. Foreign postmark. Briefing 1600, take off 1900. For real.

Teddy reads Henryk's letter as Wellington's prepared outside on his aerodrome and Spitfires being assembled in his father's factory near Leeds.

HENRYK V.O

'My dear Teddy

I apologise for the infrequency of my letters now and I'm not sure when I will be able to write again after this. Vienna is a very tense city now. We hardly ever go out and I have not been very well. Father does what he can for us but there is not much grub. I try my best to help him but I'm not that much use without my specs and sometimes don't feel I deserve whatever food he can find for us. We had a letter from my sister who is so grateful to your family for all you are doing for her, for us. One day I hope I too will be in England. I don't know if your R A F would consider me with my eyesight. Bomb aimer, perhaps..'

TEDDY (Comments)

Good old, Henry

HENRYK V.O

'..I will write again when I can. Please give my best wishes to your parents. I am glad my sister will be with you for your festival of Christmas.

Keep safe in your kite'

ADJUTANT

Girl in every port, eh, Lambert. (He looks again at postmark) Took so long to get here be quicker to drop in and pick her up yourself, mind you with your lots navigation…Now move yourself to that briefing room. For real.

Teddy folds letter, grabs flying gear and moves to briefing room.

INT. LAMBERT'S DINING ROOM - CHRISTMAS DAY 1939

Terence and Ingrid, Greta and Ilse, Mavis, Teddy and Cynthia at Christmas dinner

MAVIS

Jolly decent of you to ask me, old girl.

ILSE

More than enough for everyone, well enough greens that is.

CYNTHIA

Crackers?

ILSE

Excuse me.

CYNTHIA

Don't you have these in Germany?

ILSE

I wouldn't know

TEDDY

Cyn's wicked, but what a cracker.

INGRID

Enough of that, young man. And don't leave those carrots

TERENCE

Help you navigate at night. How are the Wellington's?

TEDDY

How are the Spits?

CYNTHIA

You boys

TEDDY

How's Henry? He's developed such a stiff upper lip I don't know what's going on with the old chap anymore.

ILSE

It is difficult to say. The red cross letters are so infrequent now. I know father will be doing his best.

INGRID

And your family, Greta. Have you heard from them since the end of August?

CYNTHIA

Come on, cheer up, might never happen.

GRETA

What do you mean might never happen?

CYNTHIA

Figure of speech. No offence meant I'm sure.

TEDDY

Knock it off, Cyn

TERENCE

King's speech.

They stand for national anthem.

ILSE

If Mr and Mrs Lambert have no objection why don't you play for us, Greta. You're the pianist.

GRETA

Henryk is the pianist. Remember.

ILSE

Greta, a waltz for Christmas, for Vienna, for all the family.

TERENCE

Yes, a toast, absent friends

GRETA

They are not friends, they are family.

ILSE

Come on, Greta. It's Christmas.

GRETA

Christmas? What's it to us, bossy boots. Christmas nothing.

CYNTHIA

Hark, laugh a minute. Smashing.

TEDDY

I told you, Cyn, knock it off.

Mavis gets Ilse up for a waltz.

TERENCE

Good idea, Ingrid may I have the pleasure.

TEDDY

Cynthia

Chorus of 'Greta, Greta..'

She walks to piano, plays a few bars of J Strauss waltz* - INTERCUT

EXT. VIENNA, GOODS SECTION OF VIENNA STATION - DAY

The Stern and Auge family in a long line in snow. In distance desks set up to organise transports. Werner near one of officials stamping papers -

Greta stops playing abruptly.

INT. MAVIS IN HER MODERN NORTH LEEDS APARTMENT - DAY

MAVIS

Looking back I remember most her bravery, humour, not that irritating humour of someone who doesn't admit what is going on and wants you to know how brave they are really, but genuine bravery, care for others. It was the best Christmas I ever had, I mean it. I've had more opulent Christmases, I've had more presents, I've had better food but it was a moment. At those times you are fortunate if you know what you know at the time, not what you know when you look back. True, we ragged her about the Ilse - Elsie - Stern Trio but she got away with it, carried it off. I suppose it was the world she came from, Vienna, Haydn, Strauss, Mozart. Every new year day I tune in now, the concert from Vienna, for a few years I couldn't watch it, looked at the polka faces in the Musikverein and couldn't help myself thinking what did you do, what didn't you do, what happened to that boy on the wrong side of history, her brother, I remember they remembered him, Henryk, Henry, number three in the trio, or number one. Does it matter. They never played again that trio, not the original line up, I sang with them a few times, taught them a new repertoire - that arrangement of a Nightingale in Berkeley Square for soprano, piano, and clarinet. A different moment. I still have a few photos. Here is that what I call original Christmas, there we all are: the Lamberts, the Sterns, me, Cyn. When Elsie saw Cyn she asked to try my lipstick! I was invited again the next year, time had already moved on. So had Cynthia. Fast one, that. Christmas day was all the women. All the remaining women, Mrs Lambert, Elsie, me. Mr Lambert seemed to live at the factory. To this day I never know exactly what he did. Like Teddy, something to do with aircraft. Teddy officially listed as missing by then, Greta was killed in the blitz, on a bus between Kings Cross and Paddington, she had been visiting us in Leeds, on her way back to the Tregowans in the west country, bomb blast sharded the windows of the double decker. I do not know how Elsie dealt with it, where she found the strength. Of course at that time she still believed, believed her parents and Henryk would come. She really believed it. Hope. I have one more picture, Teddy home on leave, her birthday, 17th I think it was, he told me he wangled his precious leave to coincide with her day on purpose. You had to take your times then. We all lived on hope. Hope and veg! Her bravery was unbelievable. Quiet bravery. I still see her even today, we laugh how her family lived near a church in Vienna, St Ruperts she called it, a church they never went to, and now I live by a synagogue in North Leeds, a synagogue I have never been to. I was never called on to be brave like her. It is a privilege to know her, know the things she told me. My life was more of a straight line. Head Girl, Leeds university, I studied history, she made it, it made her. Hope, Chance, Time. Tea?

EXT. OUTSIDE LAMBERT'S HOUSE - DAY 1941

Ilse cycling off to school as postman cycling in;nothing, again.

Ilse arrives at school. Takes standard clarinet from music store. Mavis and Ilse walk into school assembly hall.

HEADMISTRESS

Today is a special day. It is Elsie's birthday. In accordance with her tradition she is giving a present to you. Music. Please welcome Elsie with our very own head girl at the piano.

Mavis begins, Ilse freezes, Mavis tries again, Ilse completely still. Headmistress indicates to Mavis to continue solo.

Ilse sits silently in headmistress' office.

EXT. THERESIENSTADT - DAY

Henryk, ill, struggling to play piano (same music as played by Mavis) with Josef on the clarinet at a concert arranged by Nazis for Red Cross inspector

INT. HEADMISTRESS OFFICE - DAY

Ilse, Ingrid and Headmistress sit silently.

INGRID

Come home, love.

Terence arrives later in air ministry car

TERENCE

Come home, Elsie, love. Friday , fish and chips, your favourite.

INGRID

Lord, how much is she expected to take.

HEADMISTRESS

Is there anything more we can do?

Mavis enters

INGRID

You are kindness itself. This is something bigger than all of us.

HEADMISTRESS

Mavis, would you be an angel and go home with Elsie and Mr and Mrs Lambert?

INGRID

Thank you. We will be alright.

MAVIS

Talk to me, old girl. Talk.

TERENCE

Come on love.

In car

How long has this been going on?

INGRID

The Red Cross letters have stopped. Greta gone in the blitz. Too much, too young.

They arrive home

Ilse sits silently by fire, doesn't eat the fish and chips. Startled by bang on door. Terence opens door, receives telegram from R A F motorcyclist. Ilse and Ingrid stand up. Terence reads it and sits down.

TERENCE (to RAF messenger)

I won't be at the works this evening. I'll be here.

Puts more coal on fire INTERCUT

INT. INSIDE WELLINGTON BOMBER OVER HAMBURG - NIGHT

Fireball in fuselage. Teddy tapping out Morse message but flames become too intense.

INT. LAMBERT'S HOUSE LEEDS - NIGHT

Terence, Ingrid and Elsie have stayed up all night, embers in fireplace, first light, Terence draws blackout curtains.

TERENCE

We have to keep believing. All of us. Survivors. Isn't that right, Elsie?

INT. THE LAMBERTS HOUSE A FEW DAYS LATER - DAY

Headmistress visits. Ilse at home in silence.

HEADMISTRESS (to Ingrid)

I must admit if anyone ever had a reason for bunking off school this takes the kuche.

Headmistresss leaving, passing postman on way out. Nothing.

HEADMISTRESS

And any news for you, Mrs Lambert?

INGRID

No, the telegram officially said missing in action. That is all.

HEADMISTRESS

These times. This deafening silence. Elsie's family, her sister, your son, what can we do?

INT. GRETA'S QUAKER FAMILY SITTING IN SILENCE - DAY

EXT. ASSEMBLY POINT OUTSIDE THERESIENSTADT - DAY

Men and women separated. Last glance between Josef, Jacob, Henryk and Helene and Magda, train leaves.

INT. ON THE TRAIN FROM THERESIENSTADT - NIGHT

JOSEF

Where are we?

JACOB

Running late for a rendez-vous?

JOSEF

That is not like you, old friend.

JACOB

I prefer truth to rumours. The Red Cross came to Theresienstadt. There was still music. This place the guard called Auschwitz, there will be no music there, crosses will not be red.

JOSEF

I'm glad I never had a faith to lose. Except music.

JACOB

People. Love. We will see the people we love again.

JOSEF

We missed our new year concert

JACOB

Our wine, our songs, our women. How is the young man, must keep his strength together for the reunion. The Ilse Stern Trio.

JOSEF

The Grete Auge Trio.

JACOB

Henryk Stern at the piano.

JOSEF

A musician. Greatness called.

JACOB

It isn't over until…all before him - musician, writer, love, life.

They sing the tune of the piece they played at Ilse'e 16th birthday. Henryk's hands move slightly to the tune.

JOSEF

He is going from us now. A son before his father. He is going before me. This now. This gift to us.

Henryk's eyes close

HENRYK

Papa, I can't see the music

JOSEF

Play it by heart, Henryk. Encore.

Bless you my son, as you bless, blessed me, all of us.

He dies in Josef's arms.

INT. LEEDS HOUSE,ILSE'S BEDROOM - NIGHT

Ilse nightmare, wakes suddenly, speaks German ('Mutti, Papa, Henryk') for first time since she has been in England, pulls down remaining planes from ceiling, sits on landing.

Voices of Terence and Ingrid downstairs

TERENCE

I know the boy is alright.

INGRID

Do you, how? Perhaps we should face it.

TERENCE

I know. I believe. It is the only way.

INGRID

You are right. I am sorry.

TERENCE

The strain is intolerable. I know. Me working all hours, the war , rationing, now Edward.

INGRID

The silence. I can't bear the silence. Edward's silence, Elsie's silence.

TERENCE

I know you are doing your best. Try to go back to sleep. Believe.

They switch off downstairs light. Ilse goes back to bed. House in darkness. Ilse can't go back to sleep. She comes downstairs. Sits in silence, fire burned out. Early morning light, Terence comes downstairs.

TERENCE

Elsie, I didn't see you there. Good morning.

She has been crying. He lights a fire. They drink tea in silence. Factory hooter.

TERENCE

I have one thing to ask you. I have a day off on Sunday. A precious day off. What did you do on Sundays in Vienna? Look, I want you to come cycling with us. Would you like that? Fresh air, open space, change.

He cycles off to work

EXT. SUNDAY LEEDS - DAY

Ilse, Terence (on tandem) and Ingrid (on Teddy's bicycle) cycle out through the industrial city into the dales. Picnic, glorious views, silence except for skylark.

ILSE

I'm sorry.

They return at dusk through countryside back to city.

EXT. LEEDS HOUSE - DAWN

Lights and fire glow illuminate house for a second before blackout. Morning curtains open, Ilse busy in kitchen before anyone is up. She prepares a breakfast for Terence and Ingrid.

TERENCE

I say, what a breakfast, a Yorkshire spread from our honorary Yorkshire girl.

Proud of you.

As he leaves for work Ingrid and Ilse clearing in kitchen. As Ilse leaving for school postman arrives.

One Red Cross letter. Gives it to Ilse. She only sees Red Cross mark and tears it open. Leaves it on kitchen table and cycles off.

INGRID

The letter!

Ingrid runs after Ilse waving the letter but she cycles away. Ingrid goes to a telephone box. At pips puts coins in.

INGRID

It's Edward. He is a POW.

INT. SCHOOL ASSEMBLY - MORNING

MAVIS

…As my successor as head girl. She has many qualities, many gifts, for music - well, take my word on that until I can prove it to you, languages, but above all courage. Courage, adaptability, making the best of things. I am asking you to vote, vote Elsie. You won't regret it.

EXT. LEEDS ALLOTMENT - DAY

Ilse picks flowers at allotment, cycles back at house. Inside Terence and Ingrid talking, there is tea and cake untouched.

TERENCE

In this country you do not open other people's letters.

INGRID

Terence

TERENCE

I am asking you for an explanation. Do you know the strain Mrs Lambert has been under. Well?

ILSE

I am sorry. I never open other people's letters. I know the rules. I saw the Red Cross mark. I thought… I thought…I didn't think.

INGRID

What did you think, Elsie.

ILSE

I am sorry. I thought there would be news.

TERENCE

There was news. About someone else. The world doesn't totally revolve around you.

INGRID

Terence. No further. It is understandable.

ILSE

I am sorry. I didn't really read the contents of the letter, well, enough to see it didn't concern my family. It was just the post mark. I made a mistake.

Ilse runs upstairs.

Ingrid brings some tea and cake upstairs. Silence, news, silence, then dance music on radio downstairs

INGRID

Come down, love

TERENCE

Your apology is accepted. I apologise for speaking sternly. We have - are - all under a strain.

ILSE

What did the letter contain? Is it Teddy, Edward?

INT. LEEDS SCHOOL ASSEMBLY/ CONCERT HALL - DAY

HEADMISTRESS

…before we move to a vote - yes this year there will be a vote rather than an appointment of head girl, we are fighting for democracy abroad, it can begin here-so the final speech from the nominees to succeed Mavis is..Elsie.

ILSE

Thank you headmistress. An honour, it has been an honour for me to come here, to be accepted, to join in. I am no different to you. Well, I did work on my accent. I am not the most popular girl in the school. I have always known that. I am me, that's it. I never took to hockey, music and modern languages were always my bag. As an outsider who came here because I wasn't wanted in my home town I must say a simple thank you for your kindness. All of you. We are living in a world at war. I hope after the war, after we win the war, that the world will be a better place. My vision is of a world parliament where everything is sorted out by negotiation,- except the tuck shop hours of course - where there are no bullies, where everyone, of whatever background, boy or girl, is equal and respected, where these Nazis who we have all fought in our own way could never even begin. I am sorry this is all a bit serious. I can't say vote for me and every day will be a holiday, I wish I knew some good jokes, but I can't make people laugh. May be when the war is over and my family are here then if I am still head girl I can introduce laughter lessons. I wonder who would teach that.

Seriously, just vote for me and everyone will be equal under the laws of the school. I better not say serious again.

She sits, silence, then applause. Headmistress supervises votes. There is a recount. Ilse indicates privately to Mavis she will withdraw.

HEADMISTRESS

The result of the elections for head girl is a tie. Under the circumstances Mavis will continue for one more term. Please welcome your new old head girl, and her plucky runner up in a performance of The Shepherd on the Rock, arranged by Elsie Stern.

Mavis starts on the piano

MAVIS

I’m ordering you to come in this time, Elsie Stern, I’m beginning to take this personally.

After the piano intro Ilse comes in but the not concert standard clarinet squeaks. Laughter. Ilse does not join the laughter and appears to be about to make a scene.

ILSE

This clarinet is not what I am used to I only had the best instruments in Vienna..

She notices Ingrid in the front row

ILSE

But this is the best clarinet in Yorkshire.

Cheers, Mavis counts in again. Applause after, headmistress leaves room, then returns.

HEADMISTRESS

The Allies have landed in France. It is the beginning of the end of the war in Europe.

Ingrid and Elsie return home by tram. Inside Terence listening to D Day news. He retunes to dance station. He dances with Ingrid, Ilse plays along on the piano. She notices a Red Cross letter on the table.

TERENCE

Would you like a glass of beer?

INGRID

Terence! She's the deputy head girl.

TERENCE

A Red Cross letter. Look at the postmark.

Ilse tries a gulp of beer and makes a face. Ingrid brings ginger beer. Ilse picks up letter holds it up to light.

ILSE

The postmarks. It has taken a year to get here, across Europe. You open it, (to Terence) you decide what to tell me.

EXT. LEEDS TOWN HALL - DAY

Terence, Ingrid, Ilse, Mavis at V E celebrations in front of Leeds town hall. Ilse silent among the crowds.

INGRID (To Terence)

I feel these crowds are too much for her. We'll take the tram. You stay a while if you wish. Your victory too.

ILSE

I am so glad Edward, Teddy, will soon be home. You have been so brave, both of you. I know I haven't been the easiest of child..daughter, when you have had this cross to bear.

INGRID

You have been as my own child. Now you are a young lady, the war is ending, life will be normal.

ILSE

Normal

INGRID

You have to believe.

ILSE

Cycling, the allotment, fish and chips, tea

INGRID

Peace

TERENCE

Now, the European war is over, when you feel the need ask me what was in that letter all that time ago.

ILSE

You have to believe. Teddy will come back.

INGRID

Teddy now is it. Yes, Edward will return. I hope your world parliament means this will never happen again, no separation, no…

Spitfire victory roll overhead

INT. THE LAMBERTS, THE FIRST CHRISTMAS AFTER THE WAR -DAY

Ilse plays carols at the piano

TEDDY

Play us something you would have played with your family at this time of year.

Momentary silence as Ilse picks up on tense.

After Stille Nacht and toast after king’s speech, Terence asleep by fire, Ingrid goes into kitchen.

ILSE

Let me help in the kitchen.

INGRID

It is fine, dear, you did all the veg.

TEDDY

Cracker?

ILSE

We’ll wake your father

TEDDY

I think he’ll sleep for 6 years.

ILSE

How did you survive?

TEDDY

How did you?

ILSE

Tea, cycling, music, tea.

TEDDY

And fresh veg. I missed those. Well, I missed more than that.

ILSE

Do you think it is better to know everything or nothing?

TEDDY

You can't compare situations. Me- wasn't that bad once I was out of the crate. No broccoli for years.

You- I don't know how you did it. Do it. I couldn't.

Psychological, stuff getting to you. I couldn't do what you do. I'm glad you were here for my mum and dad. Your mum and dad …sorry

ILSE

I am so pleased you are back.

What became of Cynthia?

TEDDY

Some people are long haul, some aren't, some wait, some can't.

ILSE

Did you miss her?

TEDDY

Who, Cyn, yes and no. Time is a strange place.

Do you want to come to Vienna with me? Reconnaissance flight?

ILSE

No

TEDDY

I'm sorry , I didn't mean to

ILSE

I mean I don't want to go to Vienna

TEDDY

Ever?

ILSE

Never say never.

They pull a cracker. They put the hats on each other, a motto falls out.

TEDDY

Cracker.

Picks up motto

'burn your bridges, cross your rivers, the past that's the shivers, the future is so far away, smile it's just another day'

I could do with a smoke.

Terence wakes up

TEDDY

Dad, I think you should show Elsie the letters. Have a cuppa. (To Ilse)I'll see you at the cinema.

TERENCE

I think port might be more our cup of tea at this moment.

INT. LOCAL CINEMA LEEDS - EVENING

Teddy and Ilse in same seats as Teddy and Cynthia earlier. Teddy smokes, his smoking is nervy rather than suave. Organ plays, the cinema manager comes on.

MANAGER

Ladies and Gentlemen, we welcome you here to the Roundhay Roxy , I am sure you are all still celebrating Peace in Europe, indeed the world. Before our main feature I must inform you of the special content of our newsreel this evening. It is film recently released from Germany, which I as manager feel it is right to show after these long years of war and our sacrifice in the name of freedom and democracy and decency but it shows scenes of unbelievable evil and the management have reached the decision that in these circumstances we can only show the film with this warning. Thank you.

TEDDY

I need a smoke.

ILSE

You are still smoking. I want to see this.

TEDDY

I assure you don't. Come on, old girl.

He escorts her out in a hurry but the film has just started and he cannot stop Ilse from seeing the first few shots of British troops entering a concentration camp.

Outside she bursts into tears. Teddy doesn't know what to do at first, but puts out cigarette and embraces her. Ilse is completely stiff.

TEDDY

I'll take you home.

ILSE

You can't. I mean we should go back, see the main feature.

TEDDY

Sure?

ILSE

Sure

They go back in. Ilse still very stiff. He is about to light another cigarette but Ilse takes his hand to stop him then takes hand away again. The main feature, a romantic film already started. They sit in silence. Ilse crying silently in the dark. They leave at end of film.

INTERCUT INT. TRAM HOME - EVENING

ILSE

Did you know of what was in that film, the newsreel?

TEDDY

Rumours. Rumours reached our camp, very late on. The Commandant there was basically decent. We heard he'd been transferred.

ILSE

You tried to protect me.

TEDDY

I tried.

He reaches for another cigarette. She takes his hand in hers.

ILSE

Stop. Our stop. I'll protect you if you protect me.

TEDDY

The war is over.

ILSE

Is it? I don't know. I can't tell.

EXT. AISLE OF LEEDS CHURCH - DAY

Winter the next year

Ingrid Teddy Ilse Mavis leave after Terence's funeral, also R A F officers / air ministry officials

TEDDY

Dad gave this to me when he was ill. I said I should give it to you immediately. Today is as good as any.

ILSE

Your father was a good man.

INGRID

Do you not think of us as your mother and father now?

Ilse opens letter with Oslo postmark in the snow of the churchyard. V.O images of the tram outside the workshop in Vienna, the tram home in Leeds, the bombed London bus of Greta, Henryk trying to play almost blind at Theresienstadt

JACOB V.O

Ilse my child, I call you child, you will be a woman now - I do not know when you will get this letter, I do not know if you should get it, I believe the truth must be told, the story must be carried, the song sung. You are a musician, Josef's daughter, Helene's daughter, Henryk's sister. They are all gone now. We live on. You carry the past, you carry them, us, but it is your future. I enclose the Red Cross documentation, just facts, there is no other way to do it. Henryk Stern died on transport from Theresienstadt 6 March 1943, Magda Auge, Helene Stern, Josef Stern died Auschwitz, all January 1944. The Quakers wrote to me about Greta. They all loved you so. I will write again, dear Ilse, the last of us…in many ways the best of us…they will live in your music, you must go on, not surviving, living…

INT. LEEDS UNIVERSITY MUSIC PLATFORM - DAY

Ilse is leading the panel judging a trio play Der Hirt auf der felsen. INTERCUT Mavis V.O.

INT. MAVIS' FLAT IN NORTH LEEDS - DAY

There is a pram in corner, same music on radio followed by Strauss from Musikverein, she turns radio down.

MAVIS

I never really knew what she knew when. Some people found her humourless, the deputy head girl. I think she poured more layers of anti-memory concrete over her head than all the concrete in Hitler's bunkers. How could anyone survive what Elsie - Ilse did, not only survive, but function, more than function.

May be deliberately not knowing is just another form of knowing. It was her choice. Life. I'm am so glad happiness found her-

Images of her and Teddy cycling, bringing veg from allotment to Ingrid, R A F officers forming a guard of honour as she and Teddy leave Leeds church on their wedding day

-There has to be some sense in the world, the arc has to be good, it might take its time but the arc has to be good. To have known her is my life's privilege.

I have one regret, shall I say confession, it was such a long time ago now. The school election for head girl. I had a casting vote. I never used it. I have never told..

Door bell rings, Ilse enters

MAVIS

I thought the plan was to pick you both up at Leeds station, if I'd known I'd..

ILSE

I didn't go in the end.

EXT. OUTSIDE VIENNA STATION - DAY

Middle age Teddy checks his position against the old photo originally sent to him by Henryk. Elderly Jacob comes out of the station. They shake hands, tram to the Stern - Auge's workshop, Tempelgasse. Workshop is now a mobile phone store. Outside they meet civic leaders, priest from St Rupert's nearby, rabbi.

Teddy and Jacob lay a memorial. They return to station. Joseph indicates airport shuttle.

FLASHBACK of burning Wellington bomber, diving, jettisoning bombs over Hamburg.

Teddy shakes his head, shows Jacob his international rail tickets, they shake hands goodbye in the waiting room as Teddy's Vienna - Cologne train called. Jacob goes to airport shuttle. Teddy journey Vienna -Cologne- Hook of Holland - London - Leeds.

INTERCUT INT. MAVIS FLAT

MAVIS

Didn't, couldn't…?

Ilse, at pram, planes hang from the hood, radio still on, radio blends into echo of old piano playing Strauss

ILSE

How is Henry, my young English gentleman?

MAVIS

He'll be waltzing in no time. I'll put the kettle on.

ILSE

Smashing.

Music: Ilse and baby HENRY react to echo piano arrangement* of Strauss Waltz

FADE.

Platform Free

CAST:

X Civil servant, man in forties**.** Gent, suit, umbrella, *Times*, briefcase.

Q Woman in thirties, hat and gloves, Quaker.

Teddy Now 16+, 'English public school boy'- from Prague!

Monika 15+, was in same school in Prague as Teddy.

+ Guard, Announcer/s (can be doubled by members of cast)

STAGE: Simple - two chairs to indicate the trains, spotlight on each chair as **X** OR **Q** OR **Teddy** OR **Monica** speak, station sign to indicate locations:
Strawberry Hill, Peterborough, Liverpool Street, Prague. 1938 - 9
Announcements on platforms / guard on, off train .

STAGING NOTE: (if possible) MONIKA IS IN HER TRAIN SEAT THROUGHOUT THE PLAY, FIRST LOOKING OUT OF WINDOW TO TRY TO CATCH LAST GLIMPSE OF PARENTS, THEN CALM, THEN LOOKING AT WATCH /PHOTO OF TEDDY, INCREASINGLY AGITATED, SEARCHLIGHT STYLE LIGHT ON HER REACHING FULL BY THE TIME SHE SPEAKS.

STATION ANNOUNCEMENT

Platform 3. Strawberry Hill, Strawberry Hill, 8 07 Victoria, calling Richmond, Clapham Junction, Battersea, Victoria.
Mind the Doors.

X ON PLATFORM

Of course I am aware it's a cliché of fiction, same train, same platform, every weekday. You can think what you want. That's the beauty of it. Free country. Even in 1939. Say it out loud. Be my guest. I rather like the rhythm blanket, HE MAKES THE SOUND OF RAILS –Da Da Daa da - the way the world is. Looking in The Times, there are many who would like my world. It isn't about to fall in. I don't think so. Where would you rather be – Berlin, Prague, Vienna, Strawberry Hill. Quite.
Some people might want to change places with me, it isn't me who wants to change places with them. Change can be over rated, routine understated. Subjective I know.
Yes I am a civil servant. Won't ask you how you knew.
I won't distract you with my name I don't think. My job is to serve the Minister.
Hoare. H O A R E. Sir. Samuel.
Home Secretary. Home sweet Home.

TRAIN ARRIVES, HE IS STANDING EXACTLY WHERE THE CARRIAGE STOPS, CAN REACH OUT FOR THE DOOR HANDLE WITHOUT MOVING. HE BOARDS. CLOSES WINDOW FROM INSIDE, READS PAPER (THE *TIMES*: HEADLINE LATEST: POGRAMS IN BERLIN, PRAGUE, VIENNA) FOR A WHILE THEN LOOKS UP.

Home from Home. I will say this however. Today, I'm part of history. No, I'm not being histrionic. Listen to this. You don't know my name. I only answer to the Minister. Hoare. I told you.
Now this is off the record. You can hear it in Commons public gallery later today. Yes, you really can just walk into Parliament if you want.
For now its privileged information.

Listen:

TAKES DOCUMENT FROM BRIEFCASE AND READS-

'In conformity with the recommendations of the Evian Conference July 1938 His Majesty's Government have had under constant examination the contribution which they could make, in respect of the United Kingdom and of the Colonial Empire, to the international effort to facilitate the admission and settlement of involuntary emigrants from Germany…The extent to which countries can be expected to receive emigrants must depend very largely upon the *conditions* in which they are able to leave their country of origin' – do you have any idea of how I sweated over that clause!? -..yes, technical,.. technical,.. yes here it is, the flourish: note to Minister, rising intonation at this point –

' Here is a chance of taking the young generation of a great people, here is a chance of mitigating to some extent the terrible suffering of their parents and their friends'

-Since 1933 we, the UK government have permitted about 11,000 men, women and children to land in this country. I foresee we will take in the next year around 10, 000 children. Maybe I am a cliché, a banality on the 8.07, I'm not asking you to look twice, I'm not asking for honours, you won't see my name in Hansard. Facilitator. I did what I could in the time that I had. I'm a middle age man, an English commuter, a civil servant: the blanket of invisibility.
I said 10,000. 10, 000 individuals, souls.
I'm not the sort to make a noise but, I say it myself, I made a difference.

2
ON ANOTHER TRAIN **Q** AND **TEDDY** SIDE BY SIDE. SHE IS READING THE GUARDIAN.

STATION ANNOUNCEMENT:

Peterborough. Platform 3. Passengers continuing to London Liverpool Street remain on this train. Passengers for London Kings Cross change here.

Q DISEMBARKS, TEDDY REMAINS ON TRAIN**.** WE NOTICE Q HAS LEFT HER BIBLE ON THE TRAIN

Q STANDING ON THE PLATFORM LOOKING DOWN THE LINE – SHE'S JUST WAVED TEDDY OFF.

Silence.

...

How long can you stand it.
How long can you go without it.
The funny thing about breaking a silence yourself is you never know how , or when, the others would break it, which direction their silence breaker would take as opposed to yours.
It couldn't go on any longer. I don't think I was the first who couldn't stand it any longer.

Silence shattered by glass

I was
almost on the next train to London. Me, the silence breaker, walking up 10 Downing Street, the big black door swinging open. Not for a head of state, a brylcreemed Hollywood star limo'd up from the Savoy. Me. A bunch of Quakers, Jews, and other outsiders , the black door closing behind us.

Mr Chamberlain , I heard a voice say – it was mine – it is time to break the silence.

With Mr Baldwin's radio appeal we can raise £500, 000. Riches. Each child, each 'Kind' we transport out, Kindertransport, – involuntary emigration from Nazi controlled territories in Home Office speak.

Silence and time. Time to do the British thing and form …a committee, an action committee, the Refugee Children's Movement, a rescue committee, where talk after silence made a difference,

10,000 differences

My only , what, regret, guilt? – is there were not more noughts on the end of that figure, but we made a difference, there could be less, a world of noughts, of nothings if we hadn't broken the silence, doing some thing. Teddy was one, one of the first of 9,999

I met him at Harwich. My pride at meeting him, this speck, this spearhead -Lord knows how many he had left behind waving him off with smiles they hoped he couldn't read - We took another train home. North. When he found his tongue he told me of another one, far to the East. Monika. I waved him off to find her . Plan was two specks would come back as one. Monika. Monika was 10,001. Silence.

3

LIGHT DOWN , Q WALKS TO A DESK SIDE OF THE STAGE WHERE Q AND X SIT OPPOSITE EACH OTHER LOOKING AT THE DOCUMENT. THE FIRST TIME TEDDY SAYS 'Monica' Q ECHOES IT TO X. ' Monika' HE WRITES A PERMIT. SHE SHAKES HANDS WITH HIM AND RETURNS TO HER 'TRAIN'. DURING MONICA'S PIECE X RETURNS TO HIS 'TRAIN' .

FADE UP LIGHT< SOUND OF TEDDY

TRAIN ANNOUNCEMENT,	…all stations to Cambridge then fast to London Liverpool Street where this train terminates.
ECHO AND FADE EFFECT …	Terminates, terminates, termi
TEDDY	PICKING UP ON FADE…Terminus, it isn't an ominous word, it's a neutral one. Stations, Railway stations, stations of the cross, HE CASUALLY PICKS UP

BIBLE LEFT ON SEAT THEN PUTS IT BACK
just depends why you're there, which stop
you get off at, course at a terminus you don't
have a choice.
It's made for you . Nice that. Sometimes.
Have a choice made for you.
'Course if I could
choose between having a choice and not
having a choice I'd always choose choice.
Wouldn't have it any other way .
NOTE THERE IS STILL A TRACE
OF GERMAN ACCENT WITH W
PRONOUNCED V.
Of course it might depend on what the choice is or
are.
Like a vanilla or chocolate ice, kiss on the lips or
cheek, being shot, gassed, burned alive, dying
quick, dying slow, dying young, dying old, dying…
[DIRECT]God, you must think me so morbid, and
so rude.
And a guest in your great country at that!
Let's start at the beginning. Teddy is the name – as
in Dexter. Cricket, lovely cricket, I want to be as
English as Test cricket, as horizontal rain, as a
rolling green steam train.
Teddy, yes Teddy. No not Edvard, or Aaron
or anything foreign. Teddy. I've been English for
nearly 6 months now.
And I love it. Course I wish Mater and
Pater were here. I'm a good son. But you can have
fun without them. May as well (SEARCHING FOR
IDIOM) er, make hay while the…while it isn't
raining. Anyway they'll be along on a later train.
That's what Pater promised at Prague
Hauptbahnhof -, sorry, old habit, old boy, - that's a
new one for me, even young men say it to each
other – old boy, I love to say it, hear it, especially if
one of my new chums says it about me.
Rather!
No, not Hauptbahnwhatever, Teddy , old
boy, rinse your mouth out, none of that German
stuff here you know, Adolf couldn't get over the
English Channel. Main Station. That's what we say,
Teddy old boy. Just supposing, really, just
supposing old Adolf could leg it, so to speak, over
the *English* Channel we'd hit him for 6 any way.

Teddy. True the choice was initially made for me. Mater and Pater saw me off at Prague main station. Pater put his arm round me – quite rare that, Dad putting his arms round me -and said in his best German- we'd always spoken German at home, that was the language in our region of Czechlosovakia – Pater put his arm round me at the station barrier and said ' Now, Edvard – Teddy that is – next time I see you you'll be the proper English Gent. Shiny shoes, toast and marmalade, Oxford marmalade, just like where the young gentlemen all study, Play up and …'his voice broke off a bit then and for one excruciating, yes excruciation – I love that one too, only just mastered in it the lower remove last week actually – for one excruciating moment I thought
Holy Moses, Old Pater's going to blub.
And what's more, and this really takes the crackers, the Mater's going to , going to kiss me, in public on the …cheek. Well at least she made the right choice there…

GUARD

Cambridge, Cambridge. Light refreshments are available on the platform. This train halts here for 15 minutes then is fast to London Liverpool Street.

T

You know the only thing about England I've not yet got the hang of is these leather straps inside the train window. STANDS UP FROM RAILWAY SEAT AND STRUGGLES WITH THE STRAP. PLAYING WITH WHAT HE THINKS IS EXTREME, DARING LANGUAGE:
Damn, damn and blast, bugger, bugger, triple bugger , AS WINDOW FLIES OPEN - Bloody Hell!

GUARD

Bloody Hell. Now, that really isn't very nice young sir, is it? I don't want to hear anymore language like that. No call for that. I've a good mind to report you to the authorities.

T

THIS SEEMS TO THROW HIM MORE THAN NECESSARY, HIS ACCENT SLIPS…
De Authorities, I mean The Authorities. I'm sorry. I want to stay this country really I do, let me stay I won't say it again. Don't tell Pater, I mean…

GUARD	My, we are in a bit of a state aren't we, young sir, No call for that, you know what the solution to that is young gentleman, don't you, what we in this country call the ultimate solution, its what'll win us the war when it comes, this solution…
T	The solution, the solution…
GUARD	Tea, nice cup of. There you go.
T	Oh, I am so sorry TAKING THE TEA THROUGH THE WINDOW I mean so grateful. PATS HIS POCKETS. Oh, bloody hell, Oh I mean, On mein Gutes Gott, oh I mean oh Dear, yes, oh dear, I haven't any money on me. You see, you see I'm meeting my…my girlfriend at Liverpool Street. My host family used my pocket money to buy my ticket and I won't have any money until I meet my girlfriend – she said she's bringing her life saving with her. GETTING BACK INTO IT. I really am most dreadfully sorry. Old boy.
GUARD	Now you're talking, sunshine. Girlfriend , eh? I can see you're a bit of the dark horse type. More of an off spinner than an opener, I shouldn't wonder. Girlfriend, old boy? What's her name then? Greta, Lana…
T	QUIETLY Monika
GUARD	Out with it, son. Faint heart never won fair Lady.
T	Monica. Monica. RECOVERS THEN ALMOST IN TEARS. Monica, Monica, Monika, MoniKa
GUARD	My, you are in deep, aren't you old boy? Good on you. Course of true love and all that. Course I was like that when I first met my Deirdre. Not quite as, well, exotic as your flame maybe, but, well, let's say the fire still burns. Talking of which, get this tea down you sharpish and BLOWS WHISTLE PUSHES UP WINDOW FROM OUTSIDE . Next stop Monica. WINKS AS WINDOW CLOSES AND WALKS BESIDE TRAIN FOR A FEW STEPS AS IT HOOTS AND PULLS AWAY

Rather!

T I do apologise. Don't know what came over me. Thought I'd dealt with it pretty damn well up to now, though I say it myself, old chap. Stiff upper lip. It has been a bit of a strain sometimes I must say. New school, new digs, all the extra language crammers and I'd rather thought Mater and Pater would be here by now. That's what they promised at Prague Main Station. Go ahead, we've a few arrangements to make here and we'll be there before you can say wicket before leg. Was a bit of a while ago and I haven't heard from them since. Never really bothered tuning in to the wireless but did hear there was a spot of bother in some of the great European capitals, Berlin, Vienna, - all the places I'll go to one day with Ma and Pa – well, no dash it all, with Monica actually – can just see us checking into a Grand Hotel on the Kurfurstendam, Double or Single, Mein Herr, ah yes double Mr and Mrs , er Smit-
Me sporting my Brittanic Majesties Bequest Blue Passport – should have all the paperwork sorted in a jiff – I love those passports, best passports in the world, people would kill to get their mitts on one, how does it go, yes..

'His Brittanic Majesty's Secretary of State requests and requires in the name of His Majesty all those whom it may concern to allow the bearer to pass freely without let or hindrance and to freely afford the bearer such assistance as may be necessary'

Fantastic! And, Mr Hitler if you touch a single beautiful hair of Monica's sublimely dark head HMS Hood will broadside you to kingdom come, to hell for what you have done.

LOOKS OUT OF WINDOW
This green and sceptred land, this England, I am so happy here now and it will be simply topping when Mater and Pater arrive and we have tea at four and they can watch me in the second – no , first eleven, And Monica, Monica. Parting is such sweet sorrow
And when we meet….

GUARD — Liverpool Street, Liverpool street, terminus, terminus, all change

T — TO GUARD, Thank you , old boy.WINDOW DOWN EASILY THIS TIME

GUARD — LOOKING AT WINDOW
Ah, you're obviously quick on the uptake, young sir WINK I'm sure young, er…

T — Monika, Monica.

GUARD — That's the one, will be..

T and GUARD/ TOGETHER — Knocked for Six, maiden bowled over

T — …Look, I say , I owe you sixpence for the char, Monica's train will be in in 23 minutes, perhaps I could drop it off at the station office. Least I could do.

GUARD — Off you go, lad. On the house. Pleasure mine. Besides we're all be up in the station office waiting for the big one.

T — The Big One?

GUARD — PM. Chamberlain. And this Adolf chappie. Come uppance time methinks. If it's what we think it is we'll rebroadcast it over the Tannoy. Keep your ears peeled. It's time. Boat train special should be due platform 3. Never keep young ladies waiting..

MONICA — ...Waiting, Waiting…

ANOUNCER PRAGUE STATION…Special train, Prague, Hook of Holland only. No disembarkation allowed. Departure pending further announcement. Repeat no disembarkation allowed

MONICA — As if I'm going to get off having waited 3 months to get on. Now I've said goodbye to Mater and Pater I can't wait to set off. I know they only want the best for me. We all wanted to travel together. England. Always wanted to go. But always wanted to go together. 'You'll love it, Monica', Dad said. He was there once or twice before all these National Socialist types made travel so wretchedly difficult. I mean if I was Prime Minister I'd make it my first policy that people, men, women, boys, girls, people who wear these stupid stars on their coats, people who don't, could come and go as they please. Variety is the salt of life. Dad was in the financial business. Went to The City. Of London. Wish I'd taken more of an interest now. Suppose its not what a pretty young girl like me – yes, pretty, and it isn't just me who thinks it if I'm any judge of character. Feminine wiles as Mater says with that Giaconda smile.

Always thought Giaconda was a snake until I sneaked off with Edvard's Oxford Dictionary and looked it up one afternoon after English class. Giaconda smile, like that painting Mona Lisa.

Yes, pretty. I noticed Edvard looking at me in class ages ago. Boys always think they are one step ahead, I suppose we pretty girls have to let them think that. He was top of the class in English, I was second. I let that happen too. Maybe one day when we've been married forever and ever I'll tell him. I always let you go first but I always made sure you never knew. Boys are so sensitive. Girls, women, are the stronger sex. Obvious really, they live longer, they survive longer in conditions of extreme adversity. Just wait and see. I mean all this trouble now, Prague, Berlin, Vienna, all this trouble caused by men – what is that word, bit coarse really but who's listening now – strutting, yes, strutting. How silly. Walking like that, legs out hand out in that ridiculous gesture shouting out the name of another ridiculous little badly shaven strutting man. Now look at all the trouble these men have caused.

So I'm on this sealed train. Oh why doesn't it start? Least I'd be on my way then. If you gotta go…

Childhood sweethearts, that's what they call Edvard and I at school and at home now that Dad let him come round after homework. Must be such a fine boy up with a name like that as Mater said, God bless her.

Sounds like something out of Goethe, very Germanic, too Germanic to be true, I shouldn't wonder. Edvard. Teddy. What does Dad call it in banking. Hedging.

May as well, double your chances. 'Course now he got to England before me he's writing wooing letters like the proper English gentleman and signing them Teddy. I hope he hasn't changed. Childhood sweetheart,
I think lover would be so much more exciting, romantic, Hollywood, yes he's my leading man, I'm his girl, the train arrives in London, fog and smoke, gas lamps, a bobby salutes on the station forecourse, 'Good Evening Miss, welcome to London,' smoke and fog clear, I see Teddy, he runs towards me and …and…

PRAGUE STATION ANNOUNCER

Platform 3, all juveniles and accompanying officials must not leave the train . I repeat must not leave the train. Await further announcements.

MONICA

Beastly. That's what I say. Beastly. I wish… I wish We'd all left Czechoslovakia last year when Pater was in London at the Bank and we could have gone as a family, even brought some money, Dad would have seen to it. Course we're just an ordinary family, that's what Dad always says, Monica, we're just an ordinary Czech German speaking educated family, I have your mother, you have Edvard – yes he actually said that, I mean I'm 15 going on 16 and he said you have Edvard.
-Almost as if he wanted it as much as I did. Edvard had these pen friends in England. Some religious faction I'd never heard of , Q as in Queue -Quakers, don't know if that's Jewish or Christian or God knows. Dad told me off when I said I don't care about religion, religion is trouble. Teddy got papers for his train, some kids in our class went too. I saw parents at the station – stiff red lip, that's the expression Teddy uses in his letters, its RAF slang and he loves showing off.
I like it really. You have to let boys show off.-

Why, oh why are we waiting?

-It was quite a sight at the station,
Parents kissing boys and girls, youngsters, teenagers almost as old as I
waving hankerchiefs, ' we'll be

along soon, enjoy
your holiday, toodle pip old fruit' or some other Ronald Coleman act they'd picked up on the pre-newsreel show we used to be allowed to see before every thing went, I don't know the exact word , haywain. I mean ' Toodle pip,' , what's wrong with 'auf wiedersehn' , I'll see you again, good enough for Marlene, good enough for me, good enough for ....

PRAGUE STATION ANNOUNCER

Stand by for further announcement. Do not, repeat do not leave the train. Anyone attempting to leave the train may be shot...

MONICA

Why, why didn't we go when Dad was in London , we could have transferred money then, now all I have is this wretched suitcase.
I'll look such a mess when I arrive in London, all day and all night on this train with these...these kids. All I have is this dress, well, at least it was Teddy's favourite, I caught him looking at me, I pretended not to notice. I'm pretty, boys look at me. It'd be better if it wasn't for the star, or if we could , you know, customise the star. Girls don't like to look like other girls. Uniforms are for boys.
Strutters.
Strutters nutters.
If only, if only the train would go. I'll see Teddy, we'll have tea with the King, Dad will come on and join a great bank in The City, Mater and I will buy hats on the Strand and be so grand. I f only we'd gone yesterday, what day was that, the first, no, the second of September ?- dashed to the station, Dad wasn't even there this time, Mater kissed me before that policeman in brown pushed her back, coarse, no manners, not like my own Gentleman Teddy. Ma said Dad was trying to transfer some money. She had this fixed smile on her face like the lipstick had dried on her lips and if she stopped smiling they'd just crack and that wouldn't do at all. I hate stiff lips. I hate this train...
If only...
What was it yesterday, seems so faraway, I've lost track of time, stay calm, remember your lessons,

work it out, let me see
….its here in his latest letter, meet

11 AM local time 3 rd September,

London Liverpool street under the clock. If this train doesn't leave Prague right now I'll never make it. Never. He'll think I don't love him. Stood him up. It'll hurt his pride. Boys are like that. He'll think…Go train, Go, please…I …

TANNOY IN LONDON AND PRAGUE STATIONS:
Standby for further announcements

M & T IN LONDON AND PRAGUE ALMOST OVERLAPPING
M ..Love Teddy, sweetheart, Why doesn't this train go?

T ..Love Monica, sweetheart, why doesn't that train arrive?

THE FOLLOWING ANNOUNCEMENTS LONDON / PRAGUE STATIONS ALMOST OVERLAP:

LONDON ANNOUNCEMENT: CONCLUDING.. 'And with regret, I have to tell you that consequently this country is at war with Germany…'

T Thank God, at last, and I'll be in the RAF in a jiff to knock that bounder Adolf into the nastiest pavilion in the sky.
HIS MACHINE GUN NOISE ECHOES X TRAIN NOISE
Dadadadadadadat-
Just gone 11 a m . Monica must be at least off Harwich by now, within His Brittanic Majesty's range, thank God.

PRAGUE ANNOUNCEMENT: This is Station Control Prague Central. All passengers on special train at platform 13 West are to disembark immediately, repeat disembark immediately and proceed to control for reallocation to trains North and East. Do not attempt to leave the armed police cordon surrounding this train.

MONICA

DISEMBARKING IN THE THRONG
...If only...if only I could find a way to tell him, I'm more than his sweetheart, I love him...I ...

T

SOUND OF STATION CLOCK CHIMING BEHIND HIM
ON 12TH CHIME...MoniKa, I'm all alone here, England is cold and lonely, I thought... I thought you loved me, you'd turn my stiff lips red, the yellow fields green, the heavy sky blue, you – the door out of this open prison, you think it's easy being here, you think it's a film set, why don't you come, come, come and try,
try it, if you don't like it we're on the next train out, I know people on the railways, I know people, I thought I knew you, sweetheart, I thought you were a girl who kept arrangements, who didn't coast into easy options,
I'd reached the skin under the lipstick.
I go through hell for you.
Thought I knew you, but you, maybe..
maybe you just stayed home...Well, old girl, it's the end of the line for us. I'll never see you
again.

LIGHTS FADE ON TRAIN SEATS:
X reading the evening paper,
T AND Q side by side,
M in her seat now in opposite direction.

PLATFORM FREE

To the Hölzelmacher family of Vienna, district 2

Platform Free by **John F King**
Developed through **Script Yorkshire** 2009 (directed Mark Smith)
& **Ilkley Playhouse Writers House** 2014 (directed Ash Caton)

10,000 children came from Berlin Prague, Vienna etc to UK in 1938-9 under the Kindertranport scheme
A statue of commemoration is at London Liverpool street station

Acknowledgements: Association of Jewish Refugees
House of Commons Library
Library of Religious Society of Friends, London
Second Generation Network

iP

Nb Pagination of Platform Free: 17/17 refers to stage version only

Suitcase: review for Voices 2014

Suitcase . Devised and directed by

Ros Merkin

Tour performance at Leeds railway station 19 November 2013.

www.hope-street.org

Suitcase is a new departure for the growing canon of dramatic repertoire on the Kindertransport: it is performed in railway stations.

First performed at the arrival station for the original trains, London Liverpool Street, in 2008, the play was packed for a major ten station Arts Council+ - funded tour on the 75th anniversary of the Kindertransport.

I arrived for the performance at Leeds station (coincidentally – or was it – the station my mother Ilse Hölzelmacher passed through on her way from Vienna to London to Yorkshire in 1939) to hear music on the concourse thronged by the busy rail travellers of another day in Leeds.

I was lucky to have a ticket for the play about to depart .The performance was a sell-out, the Leeds connection to the subject very evidently alive. I followed the music to the reception area. An official representing the Refugee Children's Movement checked my name against their list and issued me with a label, a number and a real leaflet entitled ' While you are in England: helpful information and guidance for every refugee.' Welcome to 1938.

For the next hour and twenty minutes I and my fellow audience members, all with their suitcase style labels were in a world within a world. We had arrived at Leeds station 1938 in 2013.

Suitcase is a site specific promenade theatre created by Ros and Jane Merkin and musical director Max Reinhardt dedicated to Johanna Merkin (née Hacker) who arrived in London from Vienna in December 1938. It is produced by Hope Street Limited, a University based organisation that produces cross art-form performances in unusual spaces. They have succeeded in their aim of bringing the story so vividly to life 75 years on, reaching an old and new audience of three generations.

Being issued with an authentic label and number immediately instils one of the unique features of this event, a dissolution of barriers between audience and actors and the integration of the modern station into the timeframe of the play.

In the opening scene on the concourse the mood is light. The musicians play popular songs of the day, the newly arrived children adjust to their new surroundings but memories of their parents they left in Germany, Austria, Czechoslovakia still very much with them. As our numbers on the labels are called guides take us off deeper into the station for a series of vignettes, plays within the play which dramatize angles of the Kindertransport story. Stephan from Prague must adjust quickly to the alien customs, food and language. Kurt is separated from his sister and left alone, a speck in the station. Edith in the station buffet puts down her Daily Express to voice her fears of being overwhelmed by refugees – ' why don't they look after their own?' Bill the railway porter and trade unionist 'did the right thing, not like the Mosleyites.'

Tales are told of groups and individuals- Quakers, Baldwin, Hoare – accurately blending the historical with the emotional. As the guides lead us back through the station from the mini plays to the concourse conclusion the tone becomes darker. The children realise their parents are not imminently following them, the culture shock is having a physical toll, some children fare better than others. Anger is expressed : ' do I have to be a *Kind* forever, do I always have to be grateful?'

For myself as second generation I found Suitcase challenging and moving. Walking round Leeds station with a label and number attached to my coat, as my mother must have done, was, deliberately, an unsettling experience. Another child receives a letter returned from the Red Cross in Theresienstadt explaining remaining family has been deported to Auschwitz. My mother in Yorkshire related how she had almost exactly this situation concerning my Uncle Alfons (of Vienna district II who died in Auschwitz 23 October 1944). Tears among some audience members of second and third generation suggest I am not alone in this. The play has moments of charm but does not retreat from addressing the horror which set off the Kindertransports in the first place.

This is an original, intimate and effective dramatic work, all the more powerful for not being set in a theatre but incorporating the present atomised railway station into this past.

In that 75th anniversary year of the Kindertransport the documentary highlight for me was 'My Knees Were Jumping' which director Melissa Hacker personally presented at Second Generation Network, Wiener Library, London in July 2013. In 2014, with Journey as the theme of Holocaust Memorial Day the documentaries Nicky's Family (director Matej Minac, wwwmenemshafilms.com/nickys-family) and Into the Arms of Strangers (director M J Harris, www.intothearmsofstrangers.com) will be shown.

Aptly this anniversary tour of Suitcase came full circle at London Liverpool Street station . It stands at the platform alongside arrived fiction work Kindertransport by Diane Samuels (1995) and newer plays such as My Heart in a Suitcase by Gunning Greg, Memory by Jonathan Lichtenstein, Karen's Way by Vanessa Rosenthal and Transports by Jon Welch.

Watch out for further departures at www.suitcase1938.org

+Suitcase is also supported by-

AJR

Embassy of the Federal Republic of Germany, London

Holocaust Educational Trust

Liverpool John Moores University

Refugee Council

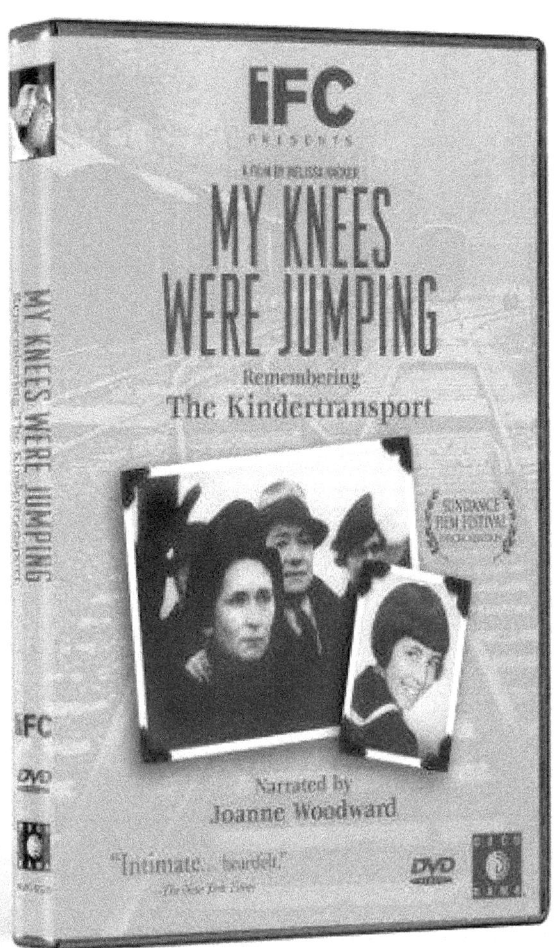
IFC
PRESENTS
MY KNEES
WERE JUMPING
Remembering
The Kindertransport
Narrated by
Joanne Woodward
"Intimate... heartfelt."
DVD

WINNER OF 12 U.S. FILM FESTIVAL AUDIENCE AWARDS!
"A MIRACLE"
Nicky's
Family
ONE ACT
OF KINDNESS
BY ONE MAN
CHANGED
THE WORLD

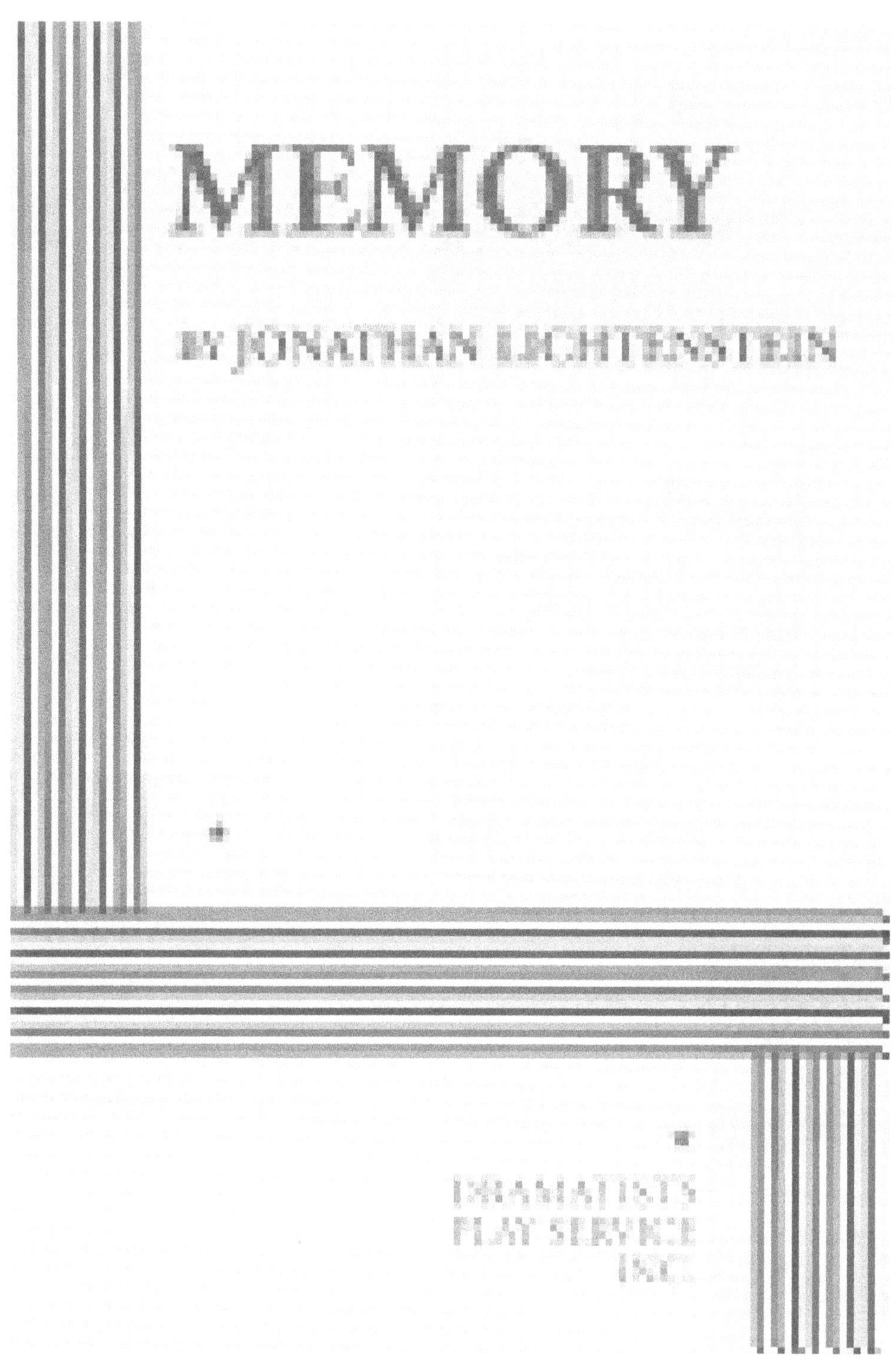

John F King is a freelance writer based in Ilkley near Leeds.

His play on this theme, title Platform Free, was recently performed at Ilkley Playhouse in 2014 and developed into screenplay Vienna, Love. ISBN 9780955851971

Jftking1@gmail.com

Review article ends

Also by **John F King** at **York European Publishing:**

Wise Guy and other fables, 2008

ISBN 9780955851902

Wise Guy, 2012, is also available as an eBook at

Smashwords ISBN 9781476351735

*Drama King, 2010

ISBN 9780955851919

A collection of drama by John King including Roundhay Ringstrasse &

Smoke a collaboration with Alan Ram

Funky / Guy and other micro-fiction, 2012

ISBN 9780955851964

Micro-Waves, 2012

ISBN 9780955851933

My 2014 review article in Second Generation Voices No 56 features some of the recent dramatic works of fiction on the Kindertransport subject.

John F King has completed creative writing courses at

Arvon

City Lit London

JBW London

Oxford University Department of Continuing Education

Script Yorkshire

Skyros Writers' Lab

UCLA (online)

York University Centre for Lifelong Learning

www.ingramcontent.com/pod-product-compliance
Ingram Content Group UK Ltd.
Pitfield, Milton Keynes, MK11 3LW, UK
UKHW050614260726
13967UKWH00008B/2868

9 780955 851971